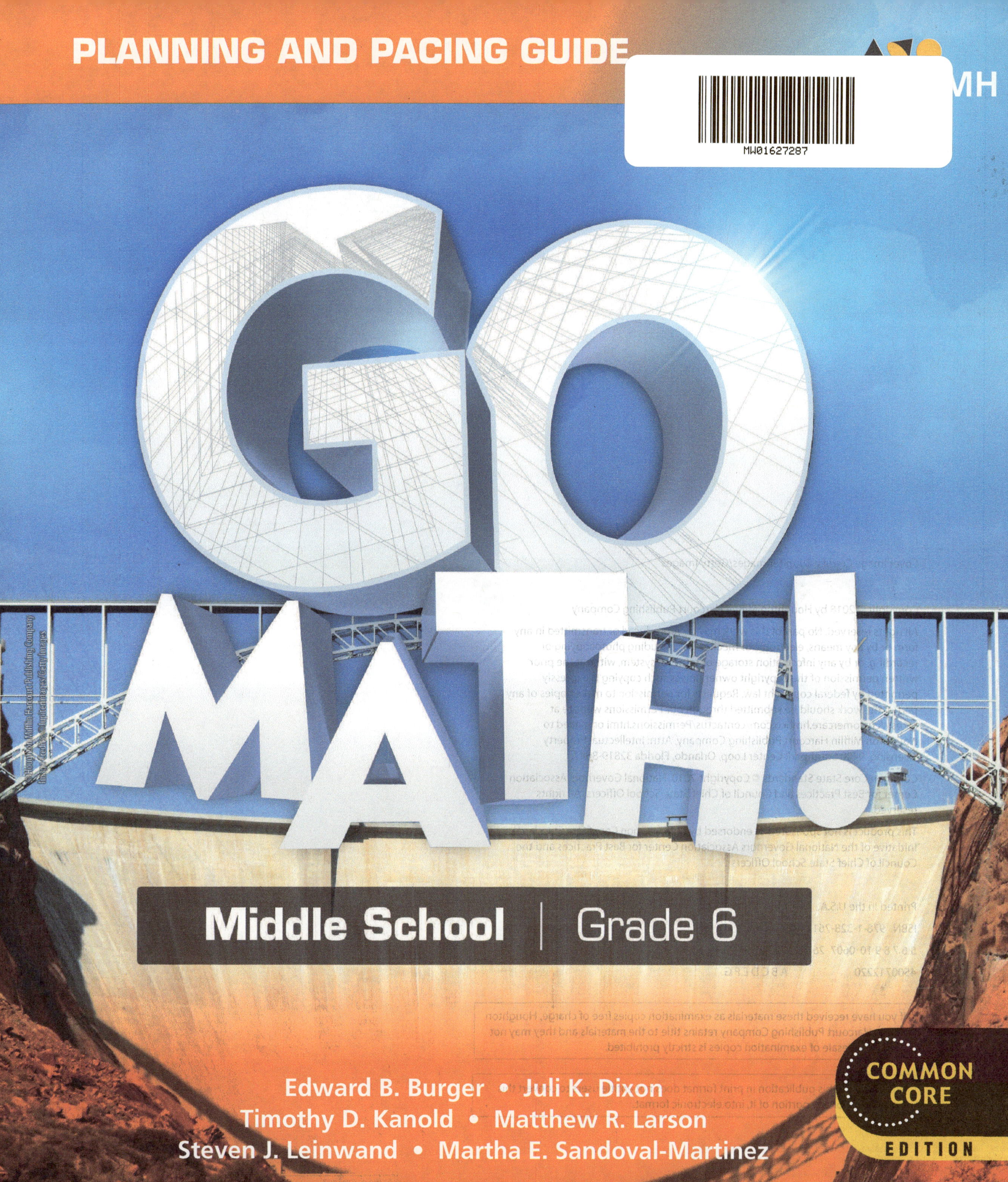
PLANNING AND PACING GUIDE
MW01627287
HMH
GO MATH!
Middle School | Grade 6
Edward B. Burger • Juli K. Dixon
Timothy D. Kanold • Matthew R. Larson
Steven J. Leinwand • Martha E. Sandoval-Martinez
COMMON CORE
EDITION

Cover Image Credits: ©Jupiterimages/Getty Images

Printed in the U.S.A.

ISBN 978-1-328-76119-4

5 6 7 8 9 10 0607 26 25 24 23 22 21 20 19 18

4500712220 A B C D E F G

Table of Contents

How to Use the Planning and Pacing Guide

Getting Your Students Ready

- *Principles of Effective Mathematics Programs* and *Mathematical Processes and Practices,* written by *Go Math* authors Dr. Juli Dixon and Dr. Matt Larson can be used as professional development in implementing *Go Math.*
- The correlation shows where every standard can be found in *Go Math*.
- Use the Pacing Guide for *Go Math* to ensure that the content assessed on the assessment is taught before the assessment is given to the students.

Go Math and the Principles of Effective Mathematics Programs

PROFESSIONAL DEVELOPMENT

by Matthew R. Larson, Ph.D.
K-12 Curriculum Specialist for Mathematics
Lincoln Public Schools
Lincoln, Nebraska

All education researchers strongly agree that two components of effective mathematics programs have a positive impact on student learning: the implemented curriculum and teachers' implementation of research-informed instructional practices.

Go Math uniquely provides both elements: a strong curriculum aligned to current expectations, and a design that robustly supports teachers' research-informed instructional practices.

Mathematical Practices Standards

PROFESSIONAL DEVELOPMENT

Developing Processes and Proficiencies in Mathematics Learners

by Juli K. Dixon, Ph.D.
Professor, Mathematics Education
University of Central Florida
Orlando, Florida

According to *Principles to Actions* (National Council of Teachers of Mathematics, 2014), "An excellent mathematics program requires effective teaching that engages students in meaningful learning through individual and collaborative experiences that promote their ability to make sense of mathematical ideas and reason mathematically" (p. 5). What this means for middle school students and how to engage students in this sort of meaningful learning is addressed in the following article.

Common Core Standards for Mathematics

COMMON CORE

Correlations for *HMH Go Math* Grade 6

Standard	Descriptor	Taught	Reinforced
6.RP RATIOS AND PROPORTIONAL RELATIONSHIPS			
Understand ratio concepts and use ratio reasoning to solve problems.			
CC.6.RP.1	Understand the concept of a ratio and use ratio language to describe a ratio relationship between two quantities.	SE: 149–150, 152	SE: 153–154, 154A–154B, 167–168, 197–198
CC.6.RP.2	Understand the concept of a unit rate $\frac{a}{b}$ associated with a ratio $a{:}b$ with $b \neq 0$, and use rate language in the context of a ratio relationship.	SE: 155–156, 158	SE: 159–160, 167–168
CC.6.RP.3	Use ratio and rate reasoning to solve real-world and mathematical problems, e.g., by reasoning about tables of equivalent ratios, tape diagrams, double number line diagrams, or equations.	SE: 151–152, 157–158, 162–164, 173, 176, 179, 182, 185–188, 193–194, 209–212, 215, 218, 220; *See also below.*	SE: 153–154, 159–160, 165–166, 167–168, 177–178, 183–184, 184A–184B, 189–190, 195–196, 197–198, 213–214, 214A–214B, 221–222, 223–224; *See also below.*
CC.6.RP.3a	Make tables of equivalent ratios relating quantities with whole-number measurements, find missing values in the tables, and plot the pairs of values on the coordinate plane. Use tables to compare ratios.	SE: 151, 161, 164, 173–176	SE: 153–154, 165–166, 177–178
CC.6.RP.3b	Solve unit rate problems including those involving unit pricing and constant speed.	SE: 155, 157–158, 175, 180–182, 193–194	SE: 159–160, 167–168, 177–178, 183–184, 184A–184B, 195–196
CC.6.RP.3c	Find a percent of a quantity as a rate per 100 (e.g., 30% of a quantity means $\frac{30}{100}$ times the quantity); solve problems involving finding the whole, given a part and the percent.	SE: 203–206, 216, 219–220	SE: 207–208, 214A–214B, 221–222, 223–224
CC.6.RP.3d	Use ratio reasoning to convert measurement units; manipulate and transform units appropriately when multiplying or dividing quantities.	SE: 185–188, 191–194	SE: 189–190, 195–196, 197–198

MAJOR CLUSTERS SUPPORTING CLUSTERS ADDITIONAL CLUSTERS

Planning and Pacing Guide CC1 Grade 6

UNIT 1

PLANNING AND PACING GUIDE

Instructional Path

Lesson	Common Core State Standards for Mathematics		Pacing*
UNIT 1 Numbers			
Progress Tracker 1 2 3 4 5 6			
MODULE 1 Integers			1 day
1.1 Identifying Integers and Their Opposites	6.NS.5	Understand that positive and negative numbers are used together to describe quantities having opposite directions or values.... *Also 6.NS.6, 6.NS.6a, 6.NS.6c*	2 days
1.2 Comparing and Ordering Integers **Going Further 1.2** Constructing Number Lines	6.NS.7b 6.NS.6	Write, interpret, and explain statements of order for rational numbers in real-world contexts. *Also 6.NS.6c, 6.NS.7, 6.NS.7a*	2 days
1.3 Absolute Value	6.NS.7c	Understand the absolute value of a rational number... Interpret absolute value as magnitude...in a real-world situation. *Also 6.NS.7, 6.NS.7d*	2 days
Ready to Go On? **Module 1 Assessment Readiness**			1 day
MODULE 2 Factors and Multiples			1 day
2.1 Greatest Common Factor	6.NS.4	Find the greatest common factor of two whole numbers....	2 days
2.2 Least Common Multiple	6.NS.4	Find the... the least common multiple of two whole numbers....	2 days
Ready to Go On? **Module 2 Assessment Readiness**			1 day
MODULE 3 Rational Numbers			1 day
3.1 Classifying Rational Numbers	6.NS.6	Understand a rational number as a point on the number line....	2 days
3.2 Identifying Opposites and Absolute Value of Rational Numbers **Activity 3.2** Magnitude Madness	6.NS.6c 6.NS.7c	Find and position integers and other rational numbers on a horizontal or vertical number line diagram.... *Also 6.NS.5, 6.NS.6, 6.NS.6a, 6.NS.7*	3 days
Getting Ready 3.3 Compare and Order 3.3 Comparing and Ordering Rational Numbers	6.NS.7a 6.NS.7a	Interpret statements of inequality.... *Also 6.NS.6, 6.NS6c, 6.NS.7, 6.NS.7b*	3 days
Ready to Go On? **Module 3 Assessment Readiness**			1 day
Study Guide Review Unit 1 Assessment Readiness			2 days

*Based on a 45-minute class period.

Major Clusters Supporting Clusters Additional Clusters

Planning and Pacing Guide CC23 Grade 6

Additional Resources for After the Assessments

End-of-Year Resources

- 20 Getting Ready lessons provide an introductory exploration of next year's content.
- Unit Projects are multiple-day culminating activities that review the standards from the current year.
- All Student materials for the End-of-Year Resources can be found online at my.hrw.com.

Go Math and the Principles of Effective Mathematics Programs

All education researchers strongly agree that two components of effective mathematics programs have a positive impact on student learning: the implemented curriculum and teachers' implementation of research-informed instructional practices.

PROFESSIONAL DEVELOPMENT

by Matthew R. Larson, Ph.D.
K-12 Curriculum Specialist for Mathematics
Lincoln Public Schools
Lincoln, Nebraska

Go Math uniquely provides both elements: a strong curriculum aligned to current expectations, and a design that robustly supports teachers' research-informed instructional practices.

The Curriculum

The power of the curriculum to affect how much students learn in mathematics is well established (Marzano, 2003; Schmoker, 2011). The National Council of Teachers of Mathematics (2014, p. 70) has argued that "an excellent mathematics program includes curriculum that develops important mathematics along coherent learning progressions."

That is precisely how we designed *HMH Go Math* Its scope and sequence are designed in accord with the latest research on learning progressions (Clements and Sarama, 2014). The curriculum makes connections between and among various mathematical topics, and it is coherent, rigorous, and focused.

The favorable outcome is that students learn each grade level's important mathematics at a deep level while simultaneously connecting each lesson to the bigger ideas of mathematics. In *HMH Go Math* an optimal proportion of the tasks students work on to develop their understanding as well as their proficiency require complex thought and reasoning – the tasks are not merely harder.

Research-Informed Instructional Practices

A coherent and rigorous curriculum is one of two critical components of a mathematics program that helps ensure the success of all students. The second critical component is an instructional approach based on research-informed instructional practices. The overarching message in NCTM's publication *Principles to Actions: Ensuring Mathematical Success for All* is that "effective teaching is the nonnegotiable core that ensures all students learn mathematics at high levels" (NCTM, 2014, p. 4). NCTM offers eight research-informed instructional strategies to support effective teaching and learning of mathematics. *HMH Go Math* embeds those eight instructional strategies in the curriculum. These strategies are shown on the following page.

Embedded Professional Development Support

As authors we appreciate that you are being asked to teach more mathematics at deeper levels than ever before. Teaching mathematics effectively is a complex endeavor, and it takes time to integrate new instructional strategies into your practice. Toward that end *HMH Go Math* embeds professional development resources into the curriculum. In a series of professional development videos, *HMH Go Math* coauthor Juli Dixon models successful teaching practices and strategies in real classrooms. These videos are an invaluable resource as you work collaboratively with your colleagues to ensure that all students successfully attain the standards and that you grow in your own knowledge of mathematics and highly effective instructional strategies.

	Instructional Strategies...	In *Go Math*...
1	**Establish mathematics goals to focus learning.** Effective teaching establishes clear goals, situates goals within learning progressions, and uses the goals to guide instructional decisions (NCTM, 2014, p. 12).	*The goals are clearly labeled in HMH Go Math. More importantly, the scope and sequence have been built around learning progressions and the big ideas of mathematics.*
2	**Implement tasks that promote reasoning and problem solving.** Effective teaching engages students in solving and discussing tasks that promote mathematical reasoning and problem solving and allow multiple entry points and varied solution strategies (NCTM, 2014, p. 17).	*The 5E lesson framework in HMH Go Math helps ensure that students explore worthwhile activities in every lesson to develop their understanding of mathematical concepts.*
3	**Use and connect mathematical representations.** Effective teaching engages students in making connections to deepen understanding of concepts and procedures and as tools for problem solving (NCTM, 2014, p. 24).	*Students interactively explore new concepts using pictorial representations, a variety of tools, and approaches in order to achieve proficiency with symbolic mathematics.*
4	**Facilitate meaningful mathematical discourse.** Effective teaching facilitates discourse among students to build shared understanding by analyzing and comparing student approaches and arguments (NCTM, 2014, p. 29).	*Math Talk is a central feature of HMH Go Math. Question prompts and sample dialogue in the Teacher Edition support you as you engage students to develop their conceptual understanding.*
5	**Pose purposeful questions.** Effective teaching uses purposeful questions to assess and advance students' reasoning and sense making (NCTM, 2014, p. 35).	*The Teacher Edition has many question prompts you can use to generate mathematical discourse and reflection, determine what students currently know, and advance their learning. These prompts allow you to transform your classroom into an interactive, student-centered learning environment.*
6	**Build procedural fluency from conceptual understanding.** Effective teaching builds fluency with procedures so that students become skillful in using procedures flexibly as they solve contextual and mathematical problems (NCTM, 2014, p. 42).	*The goal in HMH Go Math is for students to learn efficient methods for solving procedures based on understanding. Student learning of traditional algorithms starts with concrete models connected to underlying concepts. Eventually students draw their own representations and finally work with efficient algorithms so their proficiency prepares them to learn future mathematics.*
7	**Support productive struggle in learning mathematics.** Effective teaching consistently provides students with opportunities and supports to engage in productive struggle as they grapple with mathematical ideas and relationships (NCTM, 2014, p. 48).	*The 5E lesson framework supports students' continued engagement with mathematical concepts. Students have ample time to explore concepts prior to the explain phase of the lesson and are supported with significant guided practice as part of the elaborate phase.*
8	**Elicit and use evidence of student thinking.** Effective teaching uses evidence of student thinking to assess progress and to adjust instruction continually in ways that support and extend learning (NCTM, 2014, p. 53).	*Question prompts as well as Are You Ready?, Lesson Quizzes, Ready to Go On?, and Assessment Readiness in each module, and Summative Assessment options at the end of each unit provide teachers continual and real-time options to use evidence of student thinking to adjust and guide instruction. These diagnostic assessments help teachers determine the appropriate differentiated instructional materials needed to support all students.*

Mathematical Practices Standards

PROFESSIONAL DEVELOPMENT

by Juli K. Dixon, Ph.D.
Professor, Mathematics Education
University of Central Florida
Orlando, Florida

Developing Processes and Proficiencies in Mathematics Learners

According to *Principles to Actions* (National Council of Teachers of Mathematics, 2014), "An excellent mathematics program requires effective teaching that engages students in meaningful learning through individual and collaborative experiences that promote their ability to make sense of mathematical ideas and reason mathematically" (p. 5). What this means for middle school students and how to engage students in this sort of meaningful learning is addressed in the following article.

There are eight Mathematical Processes and Practices. They are based on the National Council of Teachers of Mathematics' (NCTM) *Process Standards* (NCTM, 2000) and the National Research Council's (NRC) Strands of Mathematical Proficiency (NRC, 2001). Students who are engaged in the mathematical practices around important mathematics are likely engaged in meaningful learning as described in *Principles to Actions.*

It is likely that good teachers can find evidence of each of these standards for mathematical practice in their current teaching. Regardless, it is useful to examine them and think about how each contributes to the development of mathematically proficient students. What follows is a description of how they might look in a middle school classroom. Each of these examples is reflective of experiences supported by *HMH Go Math.*

HMH Go Math supports the Mathematical Practices through several specific features including:

- Lessons focused on depth of content knowledge,
- Essential Questions to begin lessons,
- Math Talk and Questioning Strategies prompting students to use varied approaches and to explain their reasoning,
- Support for students to actively participate in their learning using write-in and/or Interactive Student Editions,
- Prompts that lead students to write their own problems or to determine if the reasoning of others is reasonable, and
- Real-world and H.O.T. problems involve students in mathematical modeling as well as logical and quantitative reasoning.

MP.1: Problem Solving

This process brings to mind developing a productive disposition as described in *Adding It Up* (NRC, 2001). In order for students to develop the diligence intended with this process, they must be provided with problems for which a pathway toward a solution is not immediately evident. If students are asked to determine the area of triangle *ABC*, a solution pathway is evident if students know the base and height of the triangle, and understand how to apply the area formula. Now, consider the same problem given the following constraints: *To find the area of a triangle ABC, Jen first drew a square around the figure. One side of the square passed through point B, one side passed through point C, and the other two sides met at point A. Draw Jen's square, and explain how you can use it to find the area of triangle ABC.*

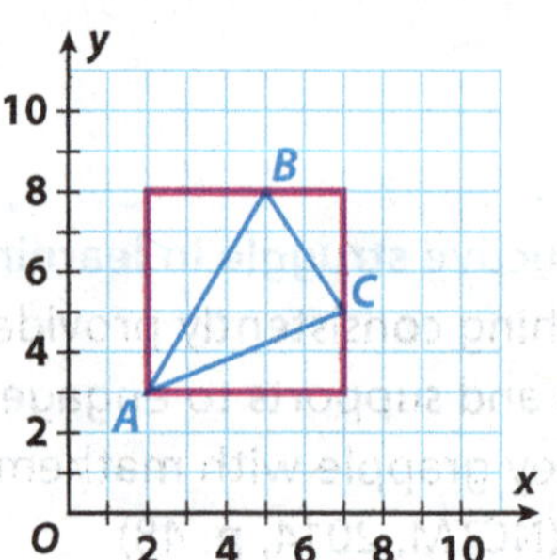

The problem is now more interesting and challenging. How will the students determine the area of triangle *ABC*, which is not a right triangle? How will the students use the area of the geometric figures that surround triangle *ABC* to solve the problem? The students will need to draw the square to make sense of the problem. The solution is within reach, but it will require diligence to persevere in reaching a solution process.

MP.2: Reason Abstractly and Quantitatively

Word problems provide important opportunities for students to make sense of mathematics around them. Students often use strategies including drawing models to make sense of a solution path. Another important strategy is for students to make sense of the problem situation by determining an equation that could represent the problem and then solving it in a mathematically proficient way. Consider the following problem: The entrance fee for Mountain World theme park is $20. Visitors purchase additional $2 tickets for rides, games, and food. The equation $y = 2x + 20$ gives the total cost, y, to visit the park, including purchasing x tickets. Draw a graph of the equation.

A student presented with this problem can use the equation to make a table of x and y-values. The student then graphs the points and connects them. The student then goes back to the problem to see that the variable x represents the number of tickets for rides, games, and food. Since partial tickets cannot be bought, it doesn't make sense to connect the points. In checking the solution for reasonableness, the student makes "sense of quantities and their relationships in problem situations" (NGA Center/CCSSO, 2010, p. 6).

MP.3: Construct Viable Arguments and Critique the Reasoning of Others

Students need to explain and justify their solution strategies. They should also listen to the explanations of other students and try to make sense of them. They will then be able to incorporate the reasoning of others into their own strategies and improve upon their own solutions. An example of this follows.

A group of students explores formulas for areas of quadrilaterals. Students make sense of the formula for the area of a parallelogram as $b \times h$ by decomposing parallelograms and composing a rectangle with the same area. Following this exploration, a student conjectures that the formula for the area of the trapezoid is also $b \times h$. The student draws this picture and says that the trapezoid can be "turned into" a rectangle with the same base by "moving one triangle over to the other side."

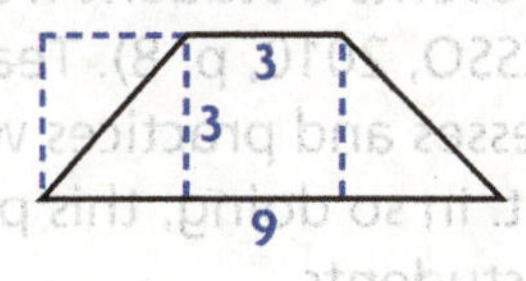

This student has constructed a viable argument based on a special type of trapezoid. Another student agrees that this formula works for an isosceles trapezoid but asks if it will also work for a general trapezoid. This second student has made sense of the reasoning of the first student and asked a question to help improve the argument.

MP.4: Model with Mathematics

Students need opportunities to use mathematics to solve real-world problems. As students learn more mathematics, the ways they model situations with mathematics should become more efficient. Consider the problem: *Jill moves her counter back 3 spaces four times, and then moves her counter forward 6 spaces.* Students first introduced to integer operations would likely model this problem with $(-3) + (-3) + (-3) + (-3) + 6$. However, a mathematically proficient student should model the same situation with $4(-3) + 6$. This demonstrates how modeling will evolve through a student's experiences in mathematics and will change as his or her understanding grows.

A useful strategy for making sense of mathematics is for students to develop real-life contexts to correspond to mathematical expressions. This supports the reflexive relationship that if a student can write a word problem for a given expression, then the student can model a similar word problem with mathematics. Consider $3(-7) - 10 + 25 = -6$. If a student is able to create a real-world context to represent this problem, then, given a word problem, the student is more likely to be able to model the word problem with mathematics and solve it.

MP.5: Use Appropriate Tools Strategically

At first glance, one might think that this practice refers to technological tools exclusively, however, tools also include paper and pencil, number lines, graphs, models, and manipulatives. Mathematically proficient students are able to determine which tool to use for a given task. An example to illustrate this practice involves multiplying fractions. A student might choose to use a number line for one problem and paper and pencil procedures for another. If presented the problem $\frac{1}{3} \times \frac{3}{4}$, a mathematically proficient student might draw a number line and divide the distance from 0 to 1 into 4 equal parts drawing a darker line through the first three fourths. That student would see that $\frac{1}{3}$ of the $\frac{3}{4}$ is $\frac{1}{4}$ of the whole. However, the same student presented with the problem $\frac{1}{3} \times \frac{4}{7}$ might not use a drawing at all, but might find it more efficient to multiply the numerators and the denominators of the factors to get $\frac{4}{21}$ as the product. Both solution paths illustrate strategic use of tools for the given problems.

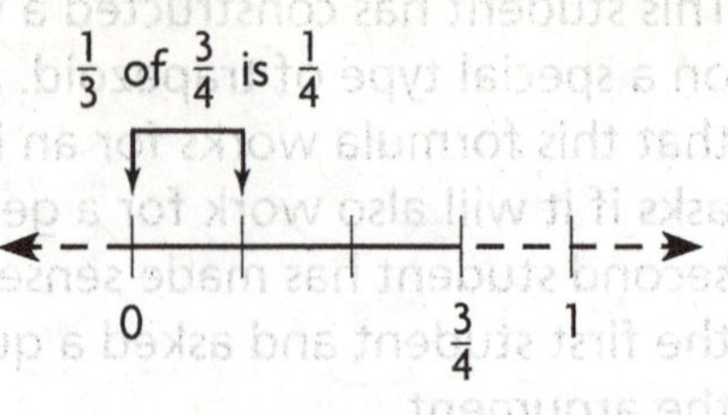

MP.6: Attend to Precision

An important aspect of precision in mathematics is developed through the language used to describe it. This can be illustrated with definitions of transformations. A student is not expected to define translations when first introduced. However, it is appropriate that students explore translations by sliding triangles to other locations on a grid. Teachers seeking to support students to attend to precision will include verbal descriptions of the slides, and require students to write rules, and then algebraic representations of those rules. These same students will be more likely to be able to correctly transform the graphs of functions in high school, because of this attention to precision when the students are in middle school.

MP.7: Look for and Make Use of Structure

Students who have made sense of strategies based on properties for finding products of single digit factors (basic facts) will be more likely to apply those properties when exploring multidigit multiplication, and later apply these properties in algebraic expressions. Consider the importance of the distributive property in looking for and making use of structure in this case. A student who has made sense of 6×7 by solving 6×5 and 6×2 has used a strategy based on the distributive property where 6×7 can be thought of as $6 \times (5 + 2)$ and then the 6 can be "distributed over" the 5 and 2. This same student can apply the distributive property to make sense of $3(x + 5) = 3 \cdot x + 3 \cdot 5 = 3x + 15$. A student who can make sense of the distributive property in this way is on a good path to making sense of the structure of algebraic expressions and equations, and the applications required to solve algebraic problems.

MP.8: Look for and Express Regularity in Repeated Reasoning

Whether performing simple calculations or solving complex problems, students should take advantage of the regularity of mathematics. If students who are exploring the volume of right rectangular prisms are given centimeter cubes and grid paper, they can build a prism with a given base and explore how the volume changes as the height of the prism increases. Students who look for ways to describe the change should see that the height of the prism is a factor of the volume of the prism and that if the area of the base is known, the volume of the prism is determined by multiplying the area of the base by the height of the prism. Identifying this pattern and repeated reasoning will help students build an understanding of the formula for the volume of right rectangular prisms.

As evidenced by the examples of mathematical processes and practices in middle school classrooms, "a lack of understanding effectively prevents a student from engaging in the mathematical practices" (NGA Center/CCSSO, 2010, p. 8). Teachers address this challenge by focusing on mathematical processes and practices while developing an understanding of the content they support. In so doing, this process facilitates the development of mathematically proficient students.

Supporting Mathematical Practices Through Questioning

When you ask…	*Students…*
• What is the problem asking? • How will you use that information? • What other information do you need? • Why did you choose that operation? • What is another way to solve that problem? • What did you do first? Why? • What can you do if you don't know how to solve a problem? • Have you solved a problem similar to this one? • When did you realize your first method would not work for this problem? • How do you know your answer makes sense?	Make sense of problems and persevere in solving them.
• What is a situation that could be represented by this equation? • What operation did you use to represent the situation? • Why does that operation represent the situation? • What properties did you use to find the answer? • How do you know your answer is reasonable?	Reason abstractly and quantitatively.
• Will that method always work? • How do you know? • What do you think about what she said? • Who can tell us about a different method? • What do you think will happen if…? • When would that not be true? • Why do you agree/disagree with what he said? • What do you want to ask her about that method? • How does that drawing support your work?	Construct viable arguments and critique the reasoning of others.

Supporting Mathematical Practices Through Questioning

When you ask…	Students…
• Why is that a good model for this problem? • How can you use a simpler problem to help you find the answer? • What conclusions can you make from your model? • How would you change your model if…?	Model with mathematics.
• What could you use to help you solve the problem? • What strategy could you use to make that calculation easier? • How would estimation help you solve that problem? • Why did you decide to use…?	Use appropriate tools strategically.
• How do you know your answer is reasonable? • How can you use math vocabulary in your explanation? • How do you know those answers are equivalent? • What does that mean?	Attend to precision.
• How did you discover that pattern? • What other patterns can you find? • What rule did you use to make this group? • Why can you use that property in this problem? • How is that like…?	Look for and make use of structure.
• What do you remember about…? • What happens when…? • What if you…instead of…? • What might be a shortcut for…?	Look for and express regularity in repeated reasoning.

Common Core Standards for Mathematics

Correlations for *HMH Go Math* Grade 6

Standard	Descriptor	Taught	Reinforced
6.RP RATIOS AND PROPORTIONAL RELATIONSHIPS			
Understand ratio concepts and use ratio reasoning to solve problems.			
CC.6.RP.1	Understand the concept of a ratio and use ratio language to describe a ratio relationship between two quantities.	SE: 149–150, 152	SE: 153–154, 154A–154B, 167–168, 197–198
CC.6.RP.2	Understand the concept of a unit rate $\frac{a}{b}$ associated with a ratio $a{:}b$ with $b \neq 0$, and use rate language in the context of a ratio relationship.	SE: 155–156, 158	SE: 159–160, 167–168
CC.6.RP.3	Use ratio and rate reasoning to solve real-world and mathematical problems, e.g., by reasoning about tables of equivalent ratios, tape diagrams, double number line diagrams, or equations.	SE: 151–152, 157–158, 162–164, 173, 176, 179, 182, 185–188, 193–194, 209–212, 215, 218, 220; *See also below.*	SE: 153–154, 159–160, 165–166, 167–168, 177–178, 183–184, 184A–184B, 189–190, 195–196, 197–198, 213–214, 214A–214B, 221–222, 223–224; *See also below.*
CC.6.RP.3a	Make tables of equivalent ratios relating quantities with whole-number measurements, find missing values in the tables, and plot the pairs of values on the coordinate plane. Use tables to compare ratios.	SE: 151, 161, 164, 173–176	SE: 153–154, 165–166, 177–178
CC.6.RP.3b	Solve unit rate problems including those involving unit pricing and constant speed.	SE: 155, 157–158, 175, 180–182, 193–194	SE: 159–160, 167–168, 177–178, 183–184, 184A–184B, 195–196
CC.6.RP.3c	Find a percent of a quantity as a rate per 100 (e.g., 30% of a quantity means $\frac{30}{100}$ times the quantity); solve problems involving finding the whole, given a part and the percent.	SE: 203–206, 216, 219–220	SE: 207–208, 214A–214B, 221–222, 223–224
CC.6.RP.3d	Use ratio reasoning to convert measurement units; manipulate and transform units appropriately when multiplying or dividing quantities.	SE: 185–188, 191–194	SE: 189–190, 195–196, 197–198

MAJOR CLUSTERS   SUPPORTING CLUSTERS   ADDITIONAL CLUSTERS

Standard	Descriptor	Taught	Reinforced
6.NS THE NUMBER SYSTEM			
Apply and extend previous understandings of multiplication and division to divide fractions by fractions.			
■ CC.6.NS.1	Interpret and compute quotients of fractions, and solve word problems involving division of fractions by fractions, e.g., by using visual fraction models and equations to represent the problem.	SE: 84A–84B, 84C–84D, 85–88, 90A–90B, 91–94, 97–98	SE: 89–90, 90C–90D, 95–96, 99–100, 101–102
Compute fluently with multi-digit numbers and find common factors and multiples.			
■ CC.6.NS.2	Fluently divide multi-digit numbers using the standard algorithm.	SE: 107–110	SE: 111–112, 135–136
■ CC.6.NS.3	Fluently add, subtract, multiply, and divide multi-digit decimals using the standard algorithm for each operation.	SE: 113–116, 119–122, 125–128, 131–132	SE: 117–118, 123–124, 129–130, 133–134, 135–136
■ CC.6.NS.4	Find the greatest common factor of two whole numbers less than or equal to 100 and the least common multiple of two whole numbers less than or equal to 12. Use the distributive property to express a sum of two whole numbers 1–100 with a common factor as a multiple of a sum of two whole numbers with no common factor.	SE: 31–34, 37–38, 79–82	SE: 35–36, 39–40, 41–42, 83–84, 102
Apply and extend previous understandings of numbers to the system of rational numbers.			
■ CC.6.NS.5	Understand that positive and negative numbers are used together to describe quantities having opposite directions or values (e.g., temperature above/below zero, elevation above/below sea level, credits/debits, positive/negative electric charge); use positive and negative numbers to represent quantities in real-world contexts, explaining the meaning of 0 in each situation.	SE: 7	SE: 11–12, 25–26, 58A–58B, 65
■ CC.6.NS.6	Understand a rational number as a point on the number line. Extend number line diagrams and coordinate axes familiar from previous grades to represent points on the line and in the plane with negative number coordinates.	SE: 7, 10, 18A–18B, 47–50, 53, 56, 58C–58D, 332, 334; ***See also below.***	SE: 12, 17, 25–26, 51–52, 58, 65–66, 335–336, 357–358; ***See also below.***
■ CC.6.NS.6a	Recognize opposite signs of numbers as indicating locations on opposite sides of 0 on the number line; recognize that the opposite of the opposite of a number is the number itself, e.g., $-(-3) = 3$, and that 0 is its own opposite.	SE: 8–10, 54, 56	SE: 11–12, 25–26, 57–58, 66
■ CC.6.NS.6b	Understand signs of numbers in ordered pairs as indicating locations in quadrants of the coordinate plane; recognize that when two ordered pairs differ only by signs, the locations of the points are related by reflections across one or both axes.	SE: 331, 334, 401–402, 404	SE: 331A–331B, 335–336, 357–358, 405–406, 412A–412B, 413–414

■ MAJOR CLUSTERS ■ SUPPORTING CLUSTERS ■ ADDITIONAL CLUSTERS

Standard	Descriptor	Taught	Reinforced
■ CC.6.NS.6c	Find and position integers and other rational numbers on a horizontal or vertical number line diagram; find and position pairs of integers and other rational numbers on a coordinate plane.	SE: 9–10, 18A–18B, 53–54, 56, 58C–58D, 331–332, 334	SE: 17, 25–26, 58, 65–66, 331A–331B, 335–336, 357–358
■ CC.6.NS.7	Understand ordering and absolute value of rational numbers.	SE: 13–14, 16, 19, 22, 55–56, 60, 62; *See also below.*	SE: 17–18, 23–24, 25–26, 57–58, 63–64, 65–66; *See also below.*
■ CC.6.NS.7a	Interpret statements of inequality as statements about the relative position of two numbers on a number line diagram.	SE: 13, 15–16, 58C–58D, 59–62	SE: 17–18, 64
■ CC.6.NS.7b	Write, interpret, and explain statements of order for rational numbers in real-world contexts.	SE: 15–16, 61–62	SE: 17–18, 26, 63–64, 65–66
■ CC.6.NS.7c	Understand the absolute value of a rational number as its distance from 0 on the number line; interpret absolute value as magnitude for a positive or negative quantity in a real-world situation.	SE: 19–22, 55–56	SE: 23–24, 25–26, 57–58, 58A–58B
■ CC.6.NS.7d	Distinguish comparisons of absolute value from statements about order.	SE: 21–22	SE: 23–24, 25–26
■ CC.6.NS.8	Solve real-world and mathematical problems by graphing points in all four quadrants of the coordinate plane. Include use of coordinates and absolute value to find distances between points with the same first coordinate or the same second coordinate.	SE: 333–334, 403–404	SE: 335–336, 405–406, 412A–412B, 413–414
6.EE EXPRESSIONS AND EQUATIONS			
Apply and extend previous understandings of arithmetic to algebraic expressions.			
■ CC.6.EE.1	Write and evaluate numerical expressions involving whole-number exponents.	SE: 237–240, 243–246, 249–252	SE: 241–242, 247–248, 253–254, 254A–254B, 255–256, 282A–282B
■ CC.6.EE.2	Write, read, and evaluate expressions in which letters stand for numbers.	SE: See below.	SE: See below.
■ CC.6.EE.2a	Write expressions that record operations with numbers and with letters standing for numbers.	SE: 261–262, 265	SE: 266–268, 283–284, 302A–302B
■ CC.6.EE.2b	Identify parts of an expression using mathematical terms (sum, term, product, factor, quotient, coefficient); view one or more parts of an expression as a single entity.	SE: 261, 265, 279–280	SE: 266, 268, 281–282, 302A–302B
■ CC.6.EE.2c	Evaluate expressions at specific values of their variables. Include expressions that arise from formulas used in real-world problems. Perform arithmetic operations, including those involving whole-number exponents, in the conventional order when there are no parentheses to specify a particular order (Order of Operations).	SE: 269–272	SE: 273–274, 274A–274B, 282A–282B, 283–284, 388A–388B, 419

Standard	Descriptor	Taught	Reinforced
CC.6.EE.3	Apply the properties of operations to generate equivalent expressions.	SE: 276–280	SE: 281–282, 282A–282B, 283–284
CC.6.EE.4	Identify when two expressions are equivalent (i.e., when the two expressions name the same number regardless of which value is substituted into them).	SE: 263, 265, 275, 280	SE: 266–267, 281–282, 282A–282B, 283–284
Reason about and solve one-variable equations and inequalities.			
CC.6.EE.5	Understand solving an equation or inequality as a process of answering a question: which values from a specified set, if any, make the equation or inequality true? Use substitution to determine whether a given number in a specified set makes an equation or inequality true.	SE: 297, 300, 304–305, 308, 312–313, 316, 319–320, 322	SE: 302, 309, 317–318, 323–324, 343–344, 350A–350B
CC.6.EE.6	Use variables to represent numbers and write expressions when solving a real-world or mathematical problem; understand that a variable can represent an unknown number, or, depending on the purpose at hand, any number in a specified set.	SE: 264–265, 298, 300, 303, 306, 308, 311, 316, 321–322	SE: 266–268, 301–302, 309–310, 317–318, 323–324, 343–344
CC.6.EE.7	Solve real-world and mathematical problems by writing and solving equations of the form $x + p = q$ and $px = q$ for cases in which p, q and x are all non-negative rational numbers.	SE: 299–300, 302C–302F, 303, 306–308, 310A–310D, 314–316, 383–384, 386, 431–432	SE: 301–302, 309–310, 317–318, 318A–318B, 343–344, 388, 433–434
CC.6.EE.8	Write an inequality of the form $x > c$ or $x < c$ to represent a constraint or condition in a real-world or mathematical problem. Recognize that inequalities of the form $x > c$ or $x < c$ have infinitely many solutions; represent solutions of such inequalities on number line diagrams.	SE: 319, 321–322	SE: 323–324, 325–326
Represent and analyze quantitative relationships between dependent and independent variables.			
CC.6.EE.9	Use variables to represent two quantities in a real-world problem that change in relationship to one another; write an equation to express one quantity, thought of as the dependent variable, in terms of the other quantity, thought of as the independent variable. Analyze the relationship between the dependent and independent variables using graphs and tables, and relate these to the equation.	SE: 337–342, 345–348, 351–354	SE: 343–344, 349–350, 355–356, 357–358
6.G GEOMETRY			
Solve real-world and mathematical problems involving area, surface area, and volume.			
CC.6.G.1	Find the area of right triangles, other triangles, special quadrilaterals, and polygons by composing into rectangles or decomposing into triangles and other shapes; apply these techniques in the context of solving real-world and mathematical problems.	SE: 371–374, 377–380, 383–386, 389–392	SE: 375–376, 381–382, 387–388, 388A–388B, 393–394, 395–396

MAJOR CLUSTERS SUPPORTING CLUSTERS ADDITIONAL CLUSTERS

Standard	Descriptor	Taught	Reinforced
CC.6.G.2	Find the volume of a right rectangular prism with fractional edge lengths by packing it with unit cubes of the appropriate unit fraction edge lengths, and show that the volume is the same as would be found by multiplying the edge lengths of the prism. Apply the formulas $V = l\,w\,h$ and $V = b\,h$ to find volumes of right rectangular prisms with fractional edge lengths in the context of solving real-world and mathematical problems.	SE: 425–428, 431–432	SE: 412A–412B, 429–430, 433–434, 435–436
CC.6.G.3	Draw polygons in the coordinate plane given coordinates for the vertices; use coordinates to find the length of a side joining points with the same first coordinate or the same second coordinate. Apply these techniques in the context of solving real-world and mathematical problems.	SE: 407–410	SE: 411–412, 412A–412B, 413–414
CC.6.G.4	Represent three-dimensional figures using nets made up of rectangles and triangles, and use the nets to find the surface area of these figures. Apply these techniques in the context of solving real-world and mathematical problems.	SE: 419–422	SE: 423–424, 435–436
6.SP STATISTICS AND PROBABILITY			
Develop understanding of statistical variability.			
CC.6.SP.1	Recognize a statistical question as one that anticipates variability in the data related to the question and accounts for it in the answers.	SE: 469, 473	SE: 474–475
CC.6.SP.2	Understand that a set of data collected to answer a statistical question has a distribution which can be described by its center, spread, and overall shape.	SE: 471, 473	SE: 474–476
CC.6.SP.3	Recognize that a measure of center for a numerical data set summarizes all of its values with a single number, while a measure of variation describes how its values vary with a single number.	SE: 449, 452	SE: 453–454
Summarize and describe distributions.			
CC.6.SP.4	Display numerical data in plots on a number line, including dot plots, histograms, and box plots.	SE: 463, 466, 470, 473, 477–478, 480	SE: 467–468, 474–476, 481–482, 483
CC.6.SP.5a	Summarize numerical data sets in relation to their context, such as by: Reporting the number of observations.	SE: 449, 452, 477–480	SE: 453–454, 481–482
CC.6.SP.5b	Summarize numerical data sets in relation to their context, such as by: Describing the nature of the attribute under investigation, including how it was measured and its units of measurement.	SE: 450, 452, 477, 479–480	SE: 453–454, 481–482

Standard	Descriptor	Taught	Reinforced
■ **CC.6.SP.5c**	Summarize numerical data sets in relation to their context, such as by: Giving quantitative measures of center (median and/or mean) and variability (interquartile range and/or mean absolute deviation), as well as describing any overall pattern and any striking deviations from the overall pattern with reference to the context in which the data were gathered.	SE: 449–452, 455–459, 464–466, 472–473, 477, 479–480	SE: 453–454, 460–462, 467–468, 474–476, 481–482, 483–484
■ **CC.6.SP.5d**	Summarize numerical data sets in relation to their context, such as by: Relating the choice of measures of center and variability to the shape of the data distribution and the context in which the data were gathered.	SE: 451, 472–473, 477, 479–480	SE: 453–454, 475–476, 481–482

Standard	Descriptor	Citations
MP MATHEMATICAL PRACTICES STANDARDS		*The mathematical practices standards are integrated throughout the book. See, for example, the citations below.*
CC.MP.1	**Make sense of problems and persevere in solving them.** Mathematically proficient students start by explaining to themselves the meaning of a problem and looking for entry points to its solution. They analyze givens, constraints, relationships, and goals. They make conjectures about the form and meaning of the solution and plan a solution pathway rather than simply jumping into a solution attempt. They consider analogous problems, and try special cases and simpler forms of the original problem in order to gain insight into its solution. They monitor and evaluate their progress and change course if necessary. Older students might, depending on the context of the problem, transform algebraic expressions or change the viewing window on their graphing calculator to get the information they need. Mathematically proficient students can explain correspondences between equations, verbal descriptions, tables, and graphs or draw diagrams of important features and relationships, graph data, and search for regularity or trends. Younger students might rely on using concrete objects or pictures to help conceptualize and solve a problem. Mathematically proficient students check their answers to problems using a different method, and they continually ask themselves, "Does this make sense?" They can understand the approaches of others to solving complex problems and identify correspondences between different approaches.	36, 97–98, 190, 268, 302, 376, 454

■ MAJOR CLUSTERS ■ SUPPORTING CLUSTERS ■ ADDITIONAL CLUSTERS

Standard	Descriptor	Citations
CC.MP.2	**Reason abstractly and quantitatively.** Mathematically proficient students make sense of quantities and their relationships in problem situations. They bring two complementary abilities to bear on problems involving quantitative relationships: the ability to decontextualize—to abstract a given situation and represent it symbolically and manipulate the representing symbols as if they have a life of their own, without necessarily attending to their referents—and the ability to contextualize, to pause as needed during the manipulation process in order to probe into the referents for the symbols involved. Quantitative reasoning entails habits of creating a coherent representation of the problem at hand; considering the units involved; attending to the meaning of quantities, not just how to compute them; and knowing and flexibly using different properties of operations and objects.	64, 90, 193, 254, 320, 382, 462
CC.MP.3	**Construct viable arguments and critique the reasoning of others.** Mathematically proficient students understand and use stated assumptions, definitions, and previously established results in constructing arguments. They make conjectures and build a logical progression of statements to explore the truth of their conjectures. They are able to analyze situations by breaking them into cases, and can recognize and use counterexamples. They justify their conclusions, communicate them to others, and respond to the arguments of others. They reason inductively about data, making plausible arguments that take into account the context from which the data arose. Mathematically proficient students are also able to compare the effectiveness of two plausible arguments, distinguish correct logic or reasoning from that which is flawed, and—if there is a flaw in an argument—explain what it is. Elementary students can construct arguments using concrete referents such as objects, drawings, diagrams, and actions. Such arguments can make sense and be correct, even though they are not generalized or made formal until later grades. Later, students learn to determine domains to which an argument applies. Students at all grades can listen or read the arguments of others, decide whether they make sense, and ask useful questions to clarify or improve the arguments.	24, 112, 208, 248, 318, 406, 468

Standard	Descriptor	Citations
CC.MP.4	**Model with mathematics.** Mathematically proficient students can apply the mathematics they know to solve problems arising in everyday life, society, and the workplace. In early grades, this might be as simple as writing an addition equation to describe a situation. In middle grades, a student might apply proportional reasoning to plan a school event or analyze a problem in the community. By high school, a student might use geometry to solve a design problem or use a function to describe how one quantity of interest depends on another. Mathematically proficient students who can apply what they know are comfortable making assumptions and approximations to simplify a complicated situation, realizing that these may need revision later. They are able to identify important quantities in a practical situation and map their relationships using such tools as diagrams, two-way tables, graphs, flowcharts and formulas. They can analyze those relationships mathematically to draw conclusions. They routinely interpret their mathematical results in the context of the situation and reflect on whether the results make sense, possibly improving the model if it has not served its purpose.	17, 100, 215–216, 249, 324, 385, 468
CC.MP.5	**Use appropriate tools strategically.** Mathematically proficient students consider the available tools when solving a mathematical problem. These tools might include pencil and paper, concrete models, a ruler, a protractor, a calculator, a spreadsheet, a computer algebra system, a statistical package, or dynamic geometry software. Proficient students are sufficiently familiar with tools appropriate for their grade or course to make sound decisions about when each of these tools might be helpful, recognizing both the insight to be gained and their limitations. For example, mathematically proficient high school students analyze graphs of functions and solutions generated using a graphing calculator. They detect possible errors by strategically using estimation and other mathematical knowledge. When making mathematical models, they know that technology can enable them to visualize the results of varying assumptions, explore consequences, and compare predictions with data. Mathematically proficient students at various grade levels are able to identify relevant external mathematical resources, such as digital content located on a website, and use them to pose or solve problems. They are able to use technological tools to explore and deepen their understanding of concepts.	8, 91, 185, 276, 303, 371, 458

Standard	Descriptor	Citations
CC.MP.6	**Attend to precision.** Mathematically proficient students try to communicate precisely to others. They try to use clear definitions in discussion with others and in their own reasoning. They state the meaning of the symbols they choose, including using the equal sign consistently and appropriately. They are careful about specifying units of measure, and labeling axes to clarify the correspondence with quantities in a problem. They calculate accurately and efficiently, express numerical answers with a degree of precision appropriate for the problem context. In the elementary grades, students give carefully formulated explanations to each other. By the time they reach high school they have learned to examine claims and make explicit use of definitions.	13, 93, 214, 242, 336, 424, 452
CC.MP.7	**Look for and make use of structure.** Mathematically proficient students look closely to discern a pattern or structure. Young students, for example, might notice that three and seven more is the same amount as seven and three more, or they may sort a collection of shapes according to how many sides the shapes have. Later, students will see 7×8 equals the well remembered $7 \times 5 + 7 \times 3$, in preparation for learning about the distributive property. In the expression $x^2 + 9x + 14$, older students can see the 14 as 2×7 and the 9 as $2 + 7$. They recognize the significance of an existing line in a geometric figure and can use the strategy of drawing an auxiliary line for solving problems. They also can step back for an overview and shift perspective. They can see complicated things, such as some algebraic expressions, as single objects or as being composed of several objects. For example, they can see $5 - 3(x - y)^2$ as 5 minus a positive number times a square and use that to realize that its value cannot be more than 5 for any real numbers x and y.	18, 118, 214, 263–264, 311, 430, 471
CC.MP.8	**Look for and express regularity in repeated reasoning.** Mathematically proficient students notice if calculations are repeated, and look both for general methods and for shortcuts. Upper elementary students might notice when dividing 25 by 11 that they are repeating the same calculations over and over again, and conclude they have a repeating decimal. By paying attention to the calculation of slope as they repeatedly check whether points are on the line through (1, 2) with slope 3, middle school students might abstract the equation $\frac{(y-2)}{(x-1)} = 3$. Noticing the regularity in the way terms cancel when expanding $(x - 1)(x + 1)$, $(x - 1)(x^2 + x + 1)$, and $(x - 1)(x^3 + x^2 + x + 1)$ might lead them to the general formula for the sum of a geometric series. As they work to solve a problem, mathematically proficient students maintain oversight of the process, while attending to the details. They continually evaluate the reasonableness of their intermediate results.	19, 125, 149, 237, 242, 310, 378, 462

Teacher Notes

UNIT 1 Numbers

MODULE 1 Integers

CLUSTER

MODULE 2 Factors and Multiples

CLUSTER

MAJOR CLUSTERS
SUPPORTING CLUSTERS
ADDITIONAL CLUSTERS

MODULE 3 Rational Numbers

CLUSTER

MAJOR CLUSTERS ■
SUPPORTING CLUSTERS ■
ADDITIONAL CLUSTERS ■

UNIT 2 Number Operations

COMMON CORE

MODULE 4 Operations with Fractions

CLUSTER

MAJOR CLUSTERS
SUPPORTING CLUSTERS
ADDITIONAL CLUSTERS

MODULE 5

Operations with Decimals

CLUSTER

MAJOR CLUSTERS ■
SUPPORTING CLUSTERS ■
ADDITIONAL CLUSTERS ■

UNIT 3 COMMON CORE

Proportionality: Ratios and Rates

MODULE 6 Representing Ratios and Rates

CLUSTER

MODULE 7 Applying Ratios and Rates

CLUSTER

MAJOR CLUSTERS ■
SUPPORTING CLUSTERS ■
ADDITIONAL CLUSTERS ■

MODULE 8 Percents

CLUSTER

MAJOR CLUSTERS ■
SUPPORTING CLUSTERS ■
ADDITIONAL CLUSTERS ■

UNIT 4 Equivalent Expressions

MODULE 9 Generating Equivalent Numerical Expressions

CLUSTER

MODULE 10 Generating Equivalent Algebraic Expressions

CLUSTER

MAJOR CLUSTERS
SUPPORTING CLUSTERS
ADDITIONAL CLUSTERS

UNIT 5 Equations and Inequalities

COMMON CORE

MODULE 11 Equations and Relationships

MAJOR CLUSTERS ■
SUPPORTING CLUSTERS ■
ADDITIONAL CLUSTERS ■

MODULE 12

Relationships in Two Variables

MAJOR CLUSTERS ■
SUPPORTING CLUSTERS ■
ADDITIONAL CLUSTERS ■

UNIT 6 Relationships in Geometry

COMMON CORE

MODULE 13 Area and Polygons

CLUSTER

MODULE 14 Distance and Area in the Coordinate Plane

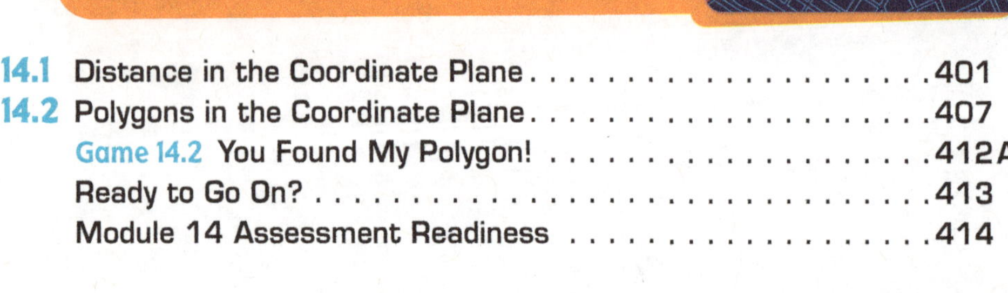

CLUSTER

MAJOR CLUSTERS
SUPPORTING CLUSTERS
ADDITIONAL CLUSTERS

MODULE 15 Surface Area and Volume of Solids

CLUSTER

MAJOR CLUSTERS ■
SUPPORTING CLUSTERS ■
ADDITIONAL CLUSTERS ■

UNIT 7 Measurement and Data

MODULE 16 Displaying, Analyzing, and Summarizing Data

CLUSTER

MAJOR CLUSTERS
SUPPORTING CLUSTERS
ADDITIONAL CLUSTERS

PLANNING AND PACING GUIDE

Instructional Path

Lesson	Common Core State Standards for Mathematics		Pacing*
UNIT 1 Numbers			
Progress Tracker 1 2 3 4 5 6			
MODULE 1 Integers			1 day
1.1 Identifying Integers and Their Opposites	**6.NS.5**	Understand that positive and negative numbers are used together to describe quantities having opposite directions or values. . . . *Also 6.NS.6, 6.NS.6a, 6.NS.6c*	2 days
1.2 Comparing and Ordering Integers **Going Further 1.2** Constructing Number Lines	**6.NS.7b** **6.NS.6**	Write, interpret, and explain statements of order for rational numbers in real-world contexts. *Also 6.NS.6c, 6.NS.7, 6.NS.7a*	2 days
1.3 Absolute Value	**6.NS.7c**	Understand the absolute value of a rational number… interpret absolute value as magnitude…in a real-world situation. *Also 6.NS.7, 6.NS.7d*	2 days
Ready to Go On? **Module 1 Assessment Readiness**			1 day
MODULE 2 Factors and Multiples			1 day
2.1 Greatest Common Factor	**6.NS.4**	Find the greatest common factor of two whole numbers. . . .	2 days
2.2 Least Common Multiple	**6.NS.4**	Find the… the least common multiple of two whole numbers. . . .	2 days
Ready to Go On? **Module 2 Assessment Readiness**			1 day
MODULE 3 Rational Numbers			1 day
3.1 Classifying Rational Numbers	**6.NS.6**	Understand a rational number as a point on the number line. . . .	2 days
3.2 Identifying Opposites and Absolute Value of Rational Numbers **Activity 3.2** Magnitude Madness	**6.NS.6c** **6.NS.7c**	Find and position integers and other rational numbers on a horizontal or vertical number line diagram. . . . *Also 6.NS.5, 6.NS.6, 6.NS.6a, 6.NS.7*	3 days
Getting Ready 3.3 Compare and Order **3.3** Comparing and Ordering Rational Numbers	**6.NS.7a** **6.NS.7a**	Interpret statements of inequality. . . . *Also 6.NS.6, 6.NS6c, 6.NS.7, 6.NS.7b*	3 days
Ready to Go On? **Module 3 Assessment Readiness**			1 day
Study Guide Review **Unit 1 Assessment Readiness**			2 days

*Based on a 45-minute class period.

Major Clusters · Supporting Clusters · Additional Clusters

PLANNING AND PACING GUIDE

Instructional Path

Lesson	Common Core State Standards for Mathematics		Pacing*
UNIT 2 Number Operations			
Progress Tracker 1 **2** 3 4 5 6 7			
MODULE 4 Operations with Fractions			**1 day**
4.1 Applying GCF and LCM to Fraction Operations **Going Further 4.1** Transforming Equations	**6.NS.4** **6.NS.1**	Find the greatest common factor of two whole numbers less than or equal to 100 and the least common multiple of two whole numbers less than or equal to 12. Use the distributive property to express a sum of two whole numbers 1–100 with a common factor as a multiple of a sum of two whole numbers with no common factor.	2 days
Getting Ready 4.2 Modeling Fraction Division **4.2** Dividing Fractions **Going Further 4.2** Real-World Division **Game 4.2** Fracto!	**6.NS.1** **6.NS.1** **6.NS.1** **6.NS.1**	Interpret and compute quotients of fractions, and solve word problems involving division of fractions by fractions, e.g., by using visual fraction models and equations to represent the problem.	4 days
4.3 Dividing Mixed Numbers	**6.NS.1**	Interpret and compute quotients of fractions, and solve word problems involving division of fractions by fractions....	2 days
4.4 Solving Multistep Problems with Fractions and Mixed Numbers	**6.NS.1**	...Solve word problems involving division of fractions by fractions....	1 day
Ready to Go On? **Module 4 Assessment Readiness**			1 day
MODULE 5 Operations with Decimals			**1 day**
5.1 Dividing Whole Numbers	**6.NS.2**	Fluently divide multi-digit numbers using the standard algorithm.	2 days
5.2 Adding and Subtracting Decimals	**6.NS.3**	Fluently add [and] subtract ... decimals using the standard algorithm....	2 days
5.3 Multiplying Decimals	**6.NS.3**	Fluently ... multiply ... multi-digit decimals using the standard algorithm....	2 days
5.4 Dividing Decimals	**6.NS.3**	Fluently ... divide multi-digit decimals using the standard algorithm....	2 days
5.5 Applying Operations with Rational Numbers	**6.NS.3**	Fluently add, subtract, multiply, and divide multi-digit decimals....	1 day
Ready to Go On? **Module 5 Assessment Readiness**			1 day
Study Guide Review **Unit 2 Assessment Readiness**			2 days

* Based on a 45-minute class period.

Major Clusters Supporting Clusters Additional Clusters

PLANNING AND PACING GUIDE

Instructional Path

Lesson		Common Core State Standards for Mathematics	Pacing*
UNIT 3 | Proportionality: Ratios and Rates			
Progress Tracker 1 2 3 4 5 6 7			
MODULE 6 | Representing Ratios and Rates			1 day
6.1 Ratios **Game 6.1** R-A-T-I-O	**6.RP.1** **6.RP.1**	Understand the concept of a ratio and use ratio language to describe a relationship between two quantities. *Also 6.RP.3, 6.RP.3a*	2 days
6.2 Rates	**6.RP.2**	Understand the concept of a unit rate a/b associated with a ratio $a:b$ with $b \neq 0$, and use rate language…. *Also 6.RP.3, 6.RP.3b*	2 days
6.3 Using Ratios and Rates to Solve Problems	**6.RP.3**	Use ratio and rate reasoning to solve… problems, e.g., by reasoning about tables… double number line diagrams…. *Also 6.RP.3a*	2 days
Ready to Go On? **Module 6 Assessment Readiness**			1 day
MODULE 7 | Applying Ratios and Rates			1 day
7.1 Ratios, Rates, Tables, and Graphs	**6.RP.3a**	Make tables of equivalent ratios…, find missing values in the tables, and plot the pairs of values on the coordinate plane…. *Also 6.RP.3, 6.RP.3b*	2 days
7.2 Solving Problems with Proportions **Game 7.2** How Fast Can You Go?	**6.RP.3** **6.RP.3b**	Use ratio and rate reasoning to solve real-world and mathematical problems, e.g., by reasoning about… equations.	2 days
7.3 Converting Within Measurement Systems	**6.RP.3d**	Use ratio reasoning to convert measurement units; manipulate and transform units appropriately when multiplying or dividing quantities. *Also 6.RP.3*	2 days
7.4 Converting Between Measurement Systems	**6.RP.3d**	Use ratio reasoning to convert measurement units; manipulate and transform units appropriately when multiplying or dividing quantities. *Also 6.RP.3, 6.RP.3b*	2 days
Ready to Go On? **Module 7 Assessment Readiness**			1 day
MODULE 8 | Percents			1 day
8.1 Understanding Percent	**6.RP.3c**	Find a percent of a quantity as a rate per 100 (e.g., 30% of a quantity means 30/100 times the quantity); ….	2 days
8.2 Percents, Fractions, and Decimals **Game 8.2** Triple Equivalence	**6.RP.3** **6.RP.3c**	Use ratio and rate reasoning to solve real-world and mathematical problems, ….	2 days
8.3 Solving Percent Problems	**6.RP.3c**	Find a percent of a quantity…; solve problems involving finding the whole, given a part and the percent. *Also 6.RP.3*	2 days
Ready to Go On? **Module 8 Assessment Readiness**			1 day
Study Guide Review **Unit 3 Assessment Readiness**			2 days

* Based on a 45-minute class period.

■ Major Clusters ■ Supporting Clusters ■ Additional Clusters

PLANNING AND PACING GUIDE

Instructional Path

Lesson	Common Core State Standards for Mathematics		Pacing*
UNIT 4 Equivalent Expressions			
Progress Tracker 1 2 3 4 5 6 7			
MODULE 9 Generating Equivalent Numerical Expressions			1 day
9.1 Exponents	**6.EE.1**	Write and evaluate numerical expressions involving whole-number exponents.	2 days
9.2 Prime Factorization	**6.EE.1**	Write and evaluate numerical expressions involving whole-number exponents.	2 days
9.3 Order of Operations **Game 9.3** Goooaaalll!	**6.EE.1** **6.EE.1**	Write and evaluate numerical expressions involving whole-number exponents.	2 days
Ready to Go On? **Module 9 Assessment Readiness**			1 day
MODULE 10 Generating Equivalent Algebraic Expressions			1 day
10.1 Modeling and Writing Expressions	**6.EE.2a**	Write expressions that record operations with numbers and with letters standing for numbers. *Also 6.EE.2b, 6.EE.4, 6.EE.6*	2 days
10.2 Evaluating Expressions **Game 10.2** Evaluate This!	**6.EE.2c** **6.EE.2c**	Evaluate expressions at specific values of their variables. Include expressions that arise from formulas used in real-world problems. Perform arithmetic operations, including those involving whole-number exponents, in the conventional order when there are no parentheses to specify a particular order (Order of Operations).	3 days
10.3 Generating Equivalent Expressions **Going Further 10.3** Equivalent Expressions	**6.EE.3** **6.EE.1**	Apply the properties of operations to generate equivalent expressions. Write and evaluate numerical expressions involving whole-number exponents. *Also 6.EE.2, 6.EE.2b, 6.EE.2c, 6.EE.4*	3 days
Ready to Go On? **Module 10 Assessment Readiness**			1 day
Study Guide Review **Unit 4 Assessment Readiness**			2 days

* Based on a 45-minute class period.

Major Clusters   Supporting Clusters   Additional Clusters

PLANNING AND PACING GUIDE

Instructional Path

Lesson	Common Core State Standards for Mathematics		Pacing*
UNIT 5 Equations and Inequalities			
Progress Tracker 1 2 3 4 5 6 7			
MODULE 11 Equations and Relationships			1 day
11.1 Writing Equations to Represent Situations **Going Further 11.1** Expressions and Equations	6.EE.7 6.EE.2a	Solve real-world problems by writing and solving equations of the form $x + p = q$ and $px = q$ for cases in which p, q, and x are all nonnegative rational numbers. *Also 6.EE.2b, 6.EE.5, 6.EE.6*	2 days
Getting Ready 11.2 Addition Equations **11.2** Addition and Subtraction Equations	6.EE.7 6.EE.7	Solve real-world problems by writing and solving equations of the form $x + p = q$ and $px = q$ for cases in which p, q, and x are all nonnegative rational numbers. *Also 6.EE.5, 6.EE.6*	2 days
Getting Ready 11.3 Multiplication Equations **11.3** Multiplication and Division Equations **Game 11.3** What is the Value?	6.EE.7 6.EE.5 6.EE.7	Understand solving an equation or inequality as a process of answering a question: which values from a specified set, if any, make the equation or inequality true? Use substitution to determine whether a given number in a specified set makes an equation or inequality true. *Also 6.EE.6*	3 days
11.4 Writing Inequalities	6.EE.8	Write an inequality of the form $x > c$ or $x < c$ to represent a constraint or condition.... *Also 6.EE.5, 6.EE.6*	2 days
Ready to Go On? **Module 11 Assessment Readiness**			1 day
MODULE 12 Relationships in Two Variables			1 day
12.1 Graphing on the Coordinate Plane **Going Further 12.1** Graphing Rational Numbers	6.NS.6c 6.NS.6b	... find and position pairs of integers and other rational numbers on a coordinate plane. *Also 6.NS.6, 6.NS.8*	2 days
12.2 Independent and Dependent Variables in Tables and Graphs	6.EE.9	... Analyze the relationship between the dependent and independent variables using graphs and tables....	3 days
12.3 Writing Equations from Tables **Game 12.3** Equation Outpost	6.EE.9 6.EE.5	... write an equation to express one quantity ... in terms of the other quantity....	2 days
12.4 Representing Algebraic Relationships in Tables and Graphs	6.EE.9	... Analyze the relationship between the dependent and independent variables using graphs and tables....	2 days
Ready to Go On? **Module 12 Assessment Readiness**			1 day
Study Guide Review **Unit 5 Assessment Readiness**			2 days

* Based on a 45-minute class period.

Major Clusters | Supporting Clusters | Additional Clusters

PLANNING AND PACING GUIDE

Instructional Path

Lesson	Common Core State Standards for Mathematics		Pacing*
UNIT 6 Relationships in Geometry			
Progress Tracker 1 2 3 4 5 6 7			
MODULE 13 Area and Polygons			**1 day**
13.1 Area of Quadrilaterals	**6.G.1**	Find the area of…special quadrilaterals, and polygons by composing into rectangles or decomposing into triangles and other shapes;… .	2 days
13.2 Area of Triangles	**6.G.1**	Find the area of right triangles, other triangles,…by composing into rectangles… .	2 days
13.3 Solving Area Equations **Activity 13.3** What is the Area?	**6.G.1** **6.G.1**	Find the area of right triangles, special quadrilaterals, and polygons…; apply these techniques in the context of solving… problems. *Also 6.EE.2c, 6.EE.7*	3 days
13.4 Area of Polygons	**6.G.1**	Find the area of…polygons by composing into rectangles or decomposing into triangles and other shapes… .	2 days
Ready to Go On? **Module 13 Assessment Readiness**			1 day
MODULE 14 Distance and Area in the Coordinate Plane			**1 day**
14.1 Distance in the Coordinate Plane	**6.NS.8**	Solve…problems by graphing points…include use of coordinates and absolute value to find distances between points… . *Also 6.NS.6b*	2 days
14.2 Polygons in the Coordinate Plane **Game 14.2** You Found My Polygon!	**6.G.3** **6.NS.6b**	Draw polygons in the coordinate plane;…find the length of a side…in the context of solving problems. *Also 6.NS.8*	3 days
Ready to Go On? **Module 14 Assessment Readiness**			1 day
MODULE 15 Surface Area and Volume of Solids			**1 day**
15.1 Nets and Surface Area	**6.G.4**	Represent three-dimensional figures using nets…and use the nets to find…surface area. *Also 6.EE.2c*	2 days
15.2 Volume of Rectangular Prisms	**6.G.2**	Find the volume of a right rectangular prism with fractional edge lengths… .	2 days
15.3 Solving Volume Equations	**6.G.2**	…Apply the formulas $V = \ell wh$ and $V = bh$ … in the context of solving real-world and mathematical problems. *Also 6.EE.7*	2 days
Ready to Go On? **Module 15 Assessment Readiness**			1 day
Study Guide Review **Unit 6 Assessment Readiness**			2 days

* Based on a 45-minute class period.

Major Clusters Supporting Clusters Additional Clusters

PLANNING AND PACING GUIDE

Instructional Path

Lesson	Common Core State Standards for Mathematics		Pacing*
UNIT 7 Measurement and Data			
Progress Tracker 1 2 3 4 5 6 7			
MODULE 16 Displaying, Analyzing, and Summarizing Data			**1 day**
16.1 Measures of Center	**6.SP.5**	Summarize numerical data sets in relation to their context. *Also 6.SP.3, 6.SP.5a, 6.SP.5b, 6.SP.5c, 6.SP.5d*	2 days
16.2 Mean Absolute Deviation	**6.SP.5c**	Summarize numerical data sets in relation to their context, such as by giving quantitative measures of center (median and/or mean) and variability (interquartile range and/or mean absolute deviation), as well as describing any overall pattern and an striking deviations from the overall pattern with reference to the context in which the data were gathered.	2 days
16.3 Box Plots	**6.SP.4**	Display numerical data in plots on a number line, including dot plots, histograms, and box plots. *Also 6.SP.5c*	2 days
16.4 Dot Plots and Data Distribution	**6.SP.4**	Display numerical data in plots on a number line, including dot plots, histograms, and box plots. *Also 6.SP.1, 6.SP.2, 6.SP.5c, 6.SP.5d*	2 days
16.5 Histograms	**6.SP.4**	Display numerical data in plots on a number line, including dot plots, histograms, and box plots. *Also 6.SP.5*	2 days
Ready to Go On? **Module 16 Assessment Readiness**			1 day
Study Guide Review **Unit 7 Assessment Readiness**			**2 days**

* Based on a 45-minute class period.

Major Clusters　Supporting Clusters　Additional Clusters

Teacher Notes

Review Projects

Unit 1 Project

EUCLID'S METHOD

Overview: In this project, students explain and demonstrate Euclid's method for finding the greatest common factor of two numbers, and they report on why Euclid was called "the Father of Geometry."

Materials: Internet access, display or poster board for presentations

Assessing Student Performance: Students' presentations should include the following information:

- A description of how to use Euclid's method to find the GCF of two numbers
- A demonstration showing how to use the method to find the GCF of 546 and 238
- A brief report explaining why Euclid is called "the Father of Geometry"

Answers

Euclid's method for finding the GCF of 546 and 238:

- $546 \div 238 = 2$, with a remainder of 70.
- $238 \div 70 = 3$, with a remainder of 28.
- $70 \div 28 = 2$, with a remainder of 14.
- $28 \div 14 = 2$, with a remainder of 0.

The GCF is 14.

Unit 1 Project

Euclid's Method

The Greek mathematician Euclid lived more than 2,000 years ago. He created a method for finding the greatest common factor of two numbers. Euclid's method for finding the GCF of 156 and 60 is shown below. No description of the steps is given, but the colors of the numbers should help you understand the method.

- $156 \div 60 = 2$, with a remainder of 36.
- $60 \div 36 = 1$, with a remainder of 24.
- $36 \div 24 = 1$, with a remainder of 12.
- $24 \div 12 = 2$, with a remainder of 0.

The last divisor is 12, so the GCF of 156 and 60 is 12.

For this project, create a presentation that includes

(1) a description of how to use Euclid's method to find the GCF of two numbers;

(2) a demonstration showing how to use the method to find the GCF of 546 and 238; and

(3) a brief report explaining why Euclid is called the "Father of Geometry."
Use the space below to write down any questions you have or important information from your teacher.

Unit 2 Project

A Fine Kettle of Fish

You have purchased an aquarium tank that is $3\frac{1}{4}$ ft long, $1\frac{1}{3}$ ft wide, and $1\frac{3}{4}$ ft tall. You plan to stock it with tropical fish. Create a presentation describing the type and number of fish you select for your aquarium. Follow these guidelines to make your decisions:

- The volume of the tank, in cubic feet, is the length times the width times the height.
- Use the rule 1 cubic foot = 7.48 gallons to find the amount of water in your tank.
- Use the rule 1 inch of fish per 2.25 gallons of water to find the total length of the fish you can safely have in your tank.
- Your aquarium must have at least 8 fish and at least 3 different species.

You can visit a store or search online for the lengths, prices, and appearances of different species of tropical fish. Your presentation should include the number and lengths of the fish you have decided to buy and the total cost of them all. Use the space below to write down any questions you have or important information from your teacher.

Unit 2 Project

A FINE KETTLE OF FISH

Overview: In this project, students apply fractions, mixed numbers, and decimal operations to decide which tropical fish they will buy for an aquarium and how much money they will spend.

Materials: Internet access, display or poster board for presentations

Assessing Student Performance: Students' presentations should include the following information:

- The total length they have calculated for all the fish in the tank
- The method they used to find the total length
- The sources of information about fish species, lengths, and prices
- The species, lengths, and prices of the fish they decided to buy
- The total cost of their fish

Answers

- Total length of fish should be about 25 in.
- Method to find total length of fish will include volume of tank (about 7.58 ft^2) times 7.48 to find capacity of tank in gallons, divided by 2.25 to find the inches of fish for the tank.

Unit 3 Project

HOW BIG IS BIG?

Overview: In this project, students use proportions to bring a large dollar amount down to earth by writing it in more easily comprehensible terms.

Materials: Internet access, display or poster board for presentations

Assessing Student Performance: Students' presentations should include the following information (amounts in parentheses give the rates per $1 million in earnings):

- The name and earnings of the celebrity/athlete that they chose and the source of the information
- The amount the person earned per hour, assuming a 40-hour, 52-week work year
- The distance the person's earnings would extend if converted to dollar bills and laid end-to-end
- The length of time it would take to spend the earnings at the rate of $1 per second
- Two additional questions and answers concerning the person's earnings

Answers

Given for $1 million per year in earnings

- Hourly rate: $480/h
- Distance: 947 ft
- Spending time @ $1/s: 11.6 days

Unit 3 Project

How Big Is Big?

Many celebrities and professional athletes make huge amounts of money each year. Is it possible to understand how big those numbers are? Choose a celebrity or athlete. Find out how much money that person earned last year. Then create a presentation that answers these questions:

- How much did the person make per hour? Assume the person worked 40 hours per week for 52 weeks.
- If the person's earnings were converted to dollar bills, how many miles would the bills stretch if they were laid end-to-end?
- How many days would it take to spend the earnings at the rate of $1 per second?

In addition to those questions, write and answer two similar questions of your own. Your questions should be aimed at converting the person's earnings into terms that are easier to understand. Use the space below to write down any questions you have or important information from your teacher.

Unit 4 Project

The Power of 2

Powers of 2 get large very quickly. It's true that 2^1 is equal to 2 and 2^2 equals just 4. But 2^{13} equals 8,192, which is slightly more than Earth's diameter in miles!

Create a presentation showing the powers of 2 from 2^0 to 2^{20}. For as many powers as possible, find a real-world distance, temperature, or length of time that is close to the power. Measurements can be in any units you choose. To get you started, place the following real-world examples with the correct powers of 2 in your presentation:

- The height of Fall Creek Falls, Tennessee, in feet
- The distance to the Moon, in miles
- The melting point of gold, in degrees Celsius

Remember: Each of your distances, temperatures, and lengths of time should be close to a power of 2 but does not have to be equal to it.

Use the space below to write down any questions you have or important information from your teacher.

Unit 4 Project

THE POWER OF 2

Overview: In this project, students calculate powers of 2 and find real-world examples with magnitudes that represent the powers.

Materials: Internet access, display or poster board for presentations

Assessing Student Performance: Students' presentations should include the following:

- The 21 powers of 2 from 2^0 to 2^{20}
- Height of Fall Creek Falls, TN, about 2^8 ft $\approx$ 256 ft
- Distance to the moon, about 2^{18} mi $\approx$ 240,000 mi
- Melting point of gold, about 2^{10}°C $\approx$ 1,064°C

Answers

The number of the remaining 18 powers for which students find approximate real-world match-ups will vary.

Powers of 2 not already given:

$2^0 = 1$	$2^1 = 2$	$2^2 = 4$
$2^3 = 8$	$2^4 = 16$	$2^5 = 32$
$2^6 = 64$	$2^7 = 128$	$2^8 = 256$
$2^9 = 512$	$2^{10} = 1{,}024$	$2^{11} = 2{,}048$
$2^{12} = 4{,}096$	$2^{13} = 8{,}192$	$2^{14} = 16{,}384$
$2^{15} = 32{,}768$	$2^{16} = 65{,}536$	$2^{17} = 131{,}072$
$2^{18} = 262{,}144$	$2^{19} = 524{,}288$	$2^{20} = 1{,}048{,}576$

Unit 5 Project

HOW FAST AND HOW FAR?

Overview: In this project, students make a table, write an equation, and draw a graph relating an animal's speed and the length of time it runs.

Materials: Internet access, graph paper, display or poster board for presentations

Assessing Student Performance: Students' presentations should include the following:

- The animal chosen, its top speed, and the source of information on the animal's speed
- A table giving *y*, the distance the animal could travel in *x* hours, for whole-number values of *x* from 0 to 10
- An equation showing the relationship between *y* and *x*
- A graph showing the relationship between *y* and *x*
- An estimation of how far the animal would run in 7 hours, 20 minutes

Unit 5 Project

How Fast and How Far?

Snails are among the slowest creatures on Earth. At top speed a snail can zip along at about 2 feet per minute. Peregrine falcons are among the fastest creatures, sometimes hitting 200 miles per hour. For this project, choose a favorite animal and find its top speed to the nearest whole number of miles per hour. Then create a presentation that includes the following:

- The source of information on the animal's speed
- A table giving *y*, the distance the animal could travel in *x* hours, for $x = 0, 1, 2, 3, 4, 5, 6, 7, 8, 9$, and 10. Assume the animal runs at its top speed for all values of *x*.
- An equation showing the relationship between *y* and *x*
- A graph showing the relationship between *y* and *x*
- An estimation, based on your graph, of how far your animal would run in 7 hours, 20 minutes, assuming top speed

Decorate your presentation with an image of your animal. Use the space below to write down any questions you have or important information from your teacher.

Unit 6 Project

Which State Is It?

Create a presentation using $8\frac{1}{2}$-by-11-inch grid paper with $\frac{1}{4}$-inch squares. Draw x- and y-axes on grid lines, dividing the page so the origin is in the middle. Plot these points and connect them to form a polygon:

(15, 17) (−2, −12) (−10, −13) (−14, −16)
(15, −12) (−2, −13) (−10, −16) (−14, 17)

You have drawn the graph of one the 50 states. Which one? Compare your graph with a map of this state, and identify as closely as you can each of the following:

- The coordinates of the state capital
- The coordinates of the state's largest city
- The coordinates of the state's only national park
- The coordinates of three other points of interest in the state

Now assume that each grid square is 12 mi^2, and use that information to answer the following questions:

- How long is the northern boundary of the state, in miles?
- How long is the western boundary of the state, in miles?
- What is the area of the state, in square miles?

Decorate your map. Use the space below to write down any questions you have or important information from your teacher.

Unit 6 Project

WHICH STATE IS IT?

Overview: In this project, students draw a map of New Mexico on the coordinate plane, plot important locations in the state, and calculate several distances and the state's area.

Materials: Internet access, $8\frac{1}{2}$-by-11-inch grid paper with $\frac{1}{4}$-inch squares, atlases or other map sources, display or poster board for presentations

Assessing Student Performance: Students' presentations should include the following:

- A map of New Mexico using the given coordinates
- The coordinates of New Mexico's capital, largest city, national park, and three other points of interest
- The lengths of the northern and western boundaries of New Mexico, and the state's area

Answers

The following coordinates are approximations:

- coordinates of state capital, Santa Fe: (2, 9)
- coordinates of largest city, Albuquerque: (−2, 6)
- coordinates of Carlsbad Caverns N.P.: (8, −11)
- length of northern boundary: 348 miles
- length of western boundary: 396 miles
- area: 124,560 sq mi

Unit 7 Project

TOP TENS

Overview: In this project, students collect data on the ten longest, tallest, widest, or fastest items in a category of interest to them and then calculate certain measures of center of the data and display the data in a box plot.

Materials: Internet access, almanacs, record books, display or poster board for presentations

Assessing Student Performance: Students' presentations should include the following:

- Ten items of data, the source where the data was found, and the reason the student chose the category
- The mean, median, mean absolute deviation, range, and outliers (if any) of the data
- A box plot of the data
- The lower quartile, the upper quartile, and the interquartile range of the data

Unit 7 Project

Top Tens

The Internet, almanacs, and record books are full of "Top 10" lists. The 10 Longest Bridges! The 10 Tallest Trees! The 10 Widest Rivers! For this project, find the Top 10 in a category that interests you. Possible areas of research are human-made structures, sports, natural objects, and geography. The only requirement is that your list must present the ten longest, tallest, widest, or fastest of something.

Then, using your ten measures as data, create a presentation that includes the following:

- Your data, including the source where you found it and the reason you chose your category
- The mean, median, mean absolute deviation, range, and outliers (if any) of your data
- A box plot of your data
- The lower quartile, the upper quartile, and the interquartile range of your data

Use the space below to write down any questions you have or important information from your teacher

Unit 7 8

Getting Ready for Grade 7 Table of Contents

Unit 8

Module GR1 Operations with Integers

Module GR2 Rational Numbers

Module GR3 Ratios and Proportional Relationships

Module GR4 Expressions, Equations, and Inequalities

GETTING READY FOR GRADE 7

GR1.1 Model Integer Addition with Same Signs

Engage

ESSENTIAL QUESTION

How can you use two-color counters to model addition of integers? Sample answer: Model the numbers with yellow counters for positive numbers or red counters for negative numbers. Then count how many counters there are in all.

Motivate the Lesson

Ask: When you model adding two integers with the same signs, will you use one color or two colors of counters?. Begin the Explore Activity to find out.

Explore

EXPLORE ACTIVITY Connect Vocabulary ELL

Help students understand the term *integers*. Review by asking students to name the numbers they count with and point out that these *counting numbers* do not include zero. Remind them that the *whole numbers* are the counting numbers and zero. Then help them understand that the whole numbers and their opposites make up the set of *integers*.

Explain

YOUR TURN Avoid Common Errors

Students may incorrectly think that the negative sign in –4 means to subtract. Explain that the sign – has two meanings: one is the *operation* of subtraction and the other is the *negative sign* for numbers to the left of zero on a number line. Demonstrate the two meanings on a calculator.

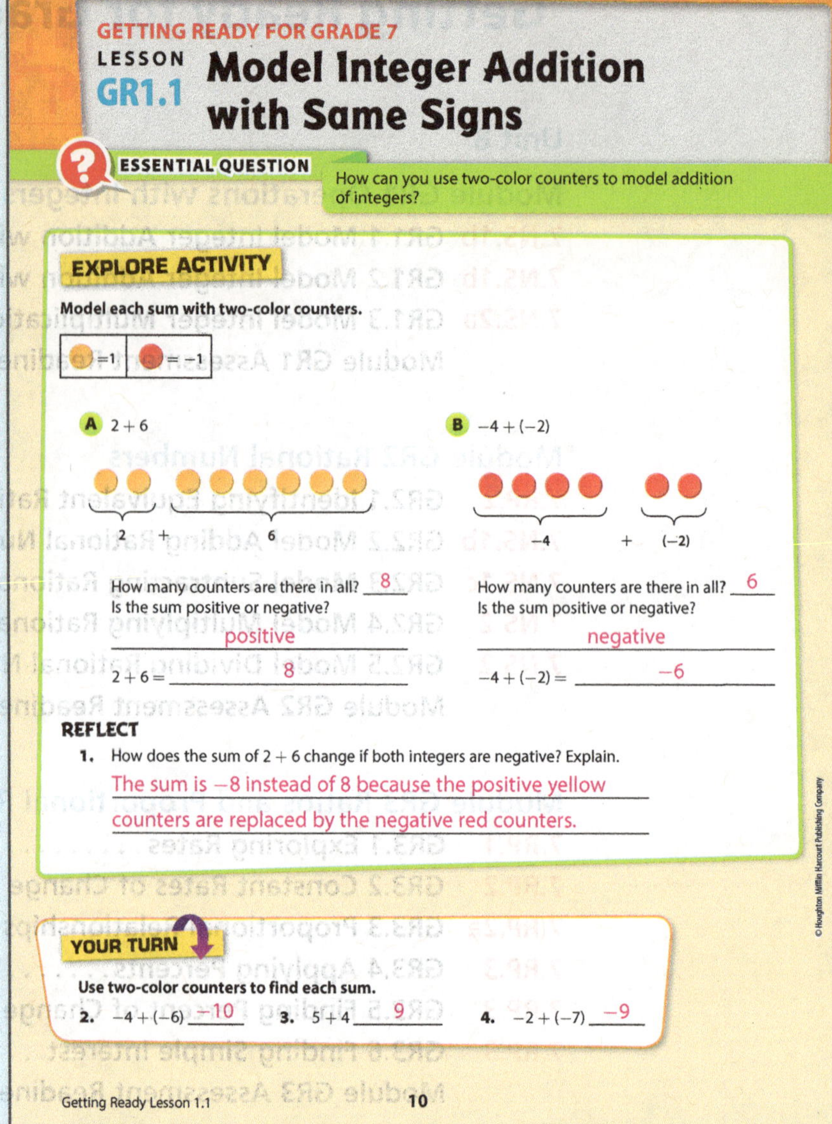

GETTING READY FOR GRADE 7

LESSON GR1.1 **Model Integer Addition with Same Signs**

ESSENTIAL QUESTION

How can you use two-color counters to model addition of integers?

EXPLORE ACTIVITY

Model each sum with two-color counters.

= 1 | = −1

A 2 + 6

2 + 6

How many counters are there in all? 8

Is the sum positive or negative? positive

2 + 6 = 8

B −4 + (−2)

−4 + (−2)

How many counters are there in all? 6

Is the sum positive or negative? negative

−4 + (−2) = −6

REFLECT

1. How does the sum of 2 + 6 change if both integers are negative? Explain.

The sum is −8 instead of 8 because the positive yellow counters are replaced by the negative red counters.

YOUR TURN

Use two-color counters to find each sum.

2. −4 + (−6) −10 3. 5 + 4 9 4. −2 + (−7) −9

© Houghton Mifflin Harcourt Publishing Company

Getting Ready Lesson 1.1 10

ADDITIONAL PRACTICE

Model each sum with two-color counters. Write the sum.

1. 4 + 3 7
2. 6 + 3 9
3. −2 + (−5) −7
4. −8 + (−2) −10
5. 1 + 9 10
6. −5 + (−4) −9
7. 7 + 2 9
8. 8 + 1 9
9. −1 + (−5) −6
10. 7 + 4 11

Guided Practice

Find each sum.

1. $5 + 4$

How many counters are there? 9

Do the counters represent positive or negative numbers? positive

$5 + 4 =$ 9

2. $-3 + (-7)$

How many counters are there? 10

Do the counters represent positive or negative numbers? negative

$-3 + (-7) =$ −10

ESSENTIAL QUESTION CHECK-IN

3. How can you use two-color counters to model addition of two positive integers?

Model the numbers with yellow and red counters. Then count how many counters there are in all. If the counters are red, the answer is negative; if they are yellow, the answer is positive.

Independent Practice

Find each sum.

4. $-4 + (-10)$ −14
5. $4 + 9$ 13
6. $-8 + (-9)$ −17
7. $42 + 16$ 58
8. $-11 + (-9)$ −20
9. $-8 + (-20)$ −28
10. $-13 + (-5)$ −18
11. $-14 + (-21)$ −35
12. $43 + 27 =$ 70

13. Jennifer has \$23 in a savings account. She deposits \$15 in the account. How much money does she have in the account now? How do you know?

\$38; Both amounts are positive and \$23 + \$15 = \$38.

14. The table shows the amount the temperature dropped in degrees Fahrenheit (°F) over four consecutive hours. What was the total drop in temperature? Explain your thinking.

Hour	1	2	3	4
Change (°F)	−2	−5	−1	−3

−11 °F; $-2 + (-5) + (-1) + (-3) = -11$

Elaborate

Talk About It Summarize the Lesson

Ask: How do you use counters to model adding integers of the same sign? If the integers are negative, model the problem using red counters to represent negative numbers. Then count the counters and write the sum as a negative number. For positive integers, model the problem using yellow counters and write the sum as a positive number.

GUIDED PRACTICE Engage with the Whiteboard

Have students model $-4 + (-7)$ and discuss what color of counter to use. Help students realize that two operation signs (+, −, ×, ÷) are never written next to each other in a math expression.

Exercise 13 Students may not understand why these amounts are represented as positive numbers. Explain that the amounts represent the money she has in her account and money that she is putting into her account.

Connect to Daily Life **Mathematical Processes and Practices**

Connect the concept of negative integers to temperatures, where a temperature dropped 3 degrees is expressed by −3, and a temperature raised 3 degrees is expressed by +3.

Evaluate

LESSON QUIZ

Find each sum.

1. $-8 + (-7)$ −15
2. $-10 + (-10)$ −20
3. $12 + 4$ 16
4. $-16 + (-2)$ −18
5. $-4 + (-15)$ −19

H.O.T. FOCUS ON HIGHER ORDER THINKING

1. **Communicate Mathematical Ideas** Which number is farther from zero on a number line, 8 or −7? Explain. 8; it is 8 units right of 0 while −7 is only 7 units left of 0. **DOK 3; MP.2**

2. **Communicate Mathematical Ideas** Which would you rather have, a debt of \$9 or a debit of \$3? Explain. \$3; −3 > −9 and a smaller debt is better. **DOK 3; MP.2**

3. **Communicate Mathematical Ideas** Which is the greater number, −9 or 3? Explain. 3; it is more units to the right on the number line than −9 **DOK 3; MP.3**

4. **Communicate Mathematical Ideas** If you were walking on a number line from −6 to +4, how many steps would you take and in which direction? 10 steps to the right **DOK 2; MP.4**

5. **Communicate Mathematical Ideas** If you were walking on a number line from −10 to −2, how many steps would you take and in which direction? 8 steps to the right **DOK 2; MP.4**

6. **Communicate Mathematical Ideas** If you were walking on a number line from 7 to −3, how many steps would you take and in which direction? 10 steps to the left **DOK 2; MP.4**

GETTING READY FOR GRADE 7

GR1.2 Model Integer Addition with Different Signs

Engage

ESSENTIAL QUESTION

How can you use a number line to model addition of integers with different signs? Start at the first integer. Move the number of units indicated by the second integer. Move to the right if the sign of the second integer is positive. Move to the left if the sign of the second integer is negative.

Motivate the Lesson

Ask: The school's science club raised $300, but spent $45 on supplies to raise the money. How can you express the actual amount earned as the sum of two integers with different signs? Begin the Explore Activity to find out.

Explore

EXPLORE ACTIVITY

Connect Vocabulary ELL

Help students understand the term *integers*. Ask students to name some numbers that are **not** integers. They may answer with examples that are fractions or decimals. Help them to see that $\frac{8}{2}$ is a fraction in *form* only, and that its *value* is the integer 4.

Explain

YOUR TURN

Avoid Common Errors

Exercise 2 Some students may forget to use the sign of the integer with the greater value. Encourage these students to check the sign on every sum.

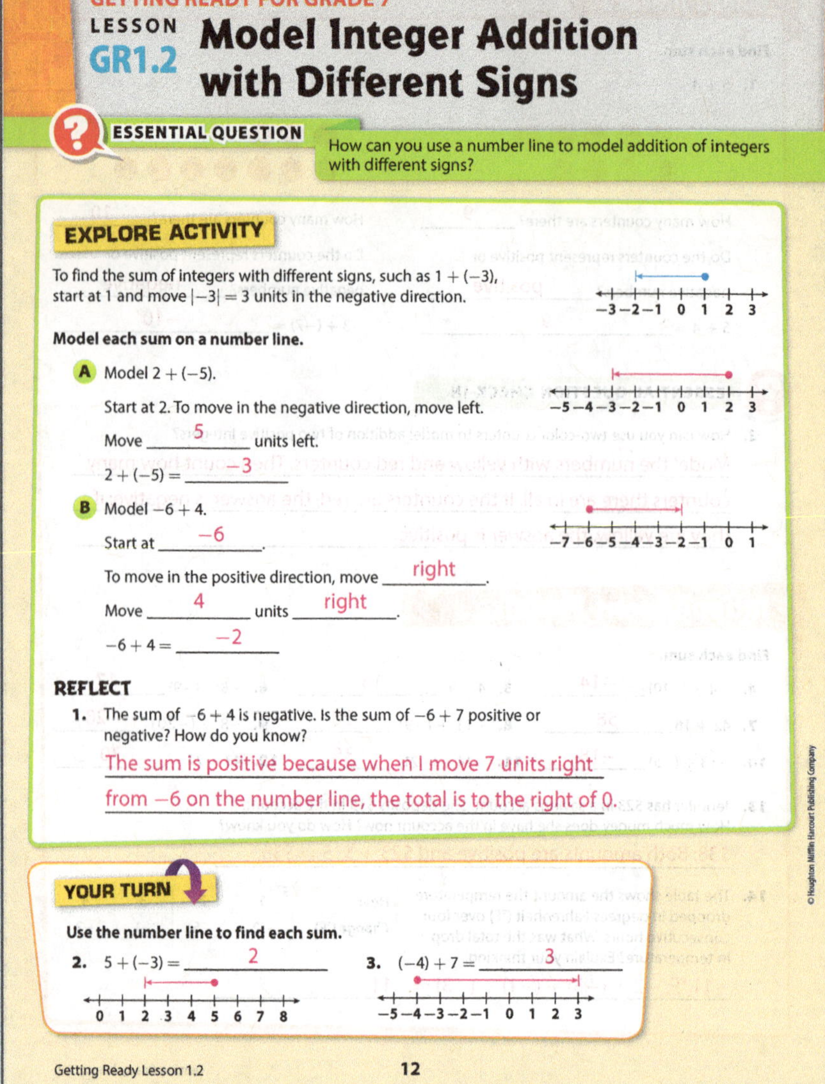
GETTING READY FOR GRADE 7

LESSON GR1.2 **Model Integer Addition with Different Signs**

ESSENTIAL QUESTION

How can you use a number line to model addition of integers with different signs?

EXPLORE ACTIVITY

To find the sum of integers with different signs, such as $1 + (-3)$, start at 1 and move $|-3| = 3$ units in the negative direction.

Model each sum on a number line.

A Model $2 + (-5)$.

Start at 2. To move in the negative direction, move left.

Move 5 units left.

$2 + (-5) =$ −3

B Model $-6 + 4$.

Start at −6.

To move in the positive direction, move right.

Move 4 units right.

$-6 + 4 =$ −2

REFLECT

1. The sum of $-6 + 4$ is negative. Is the sum of $-6 + 7$ positive or negative? How do you know?

The sum is positive because when I move 7 units right from −6 on the number line, the total is to the right of 0.

YOUR TURN

Use the number line to find each sum.

2. $5 + (-3) =$ 2

3. $(-4) + 7 =$ 3

ADDITIONAL PRACTICE

Find each sum.

1. $4 + (-3)$ 1	**2.** $6 + (-6)$ 0
3. $2 + (-5)$ −3	**4.** $1 + (-2)$ −1
5. $1 + (-9)$ −8	**6.** $-5 + 4$ −1
7. $(-7) + 2$ −5	**8.** $8 + (-1)$ 7
9. $1 + (-5)$ −4	**10.** $-7 + 4$ −3

Guided Practice

Model each sum on the number line.

1. $3 + (-3)$

Where should you start on the number line? 3

Should you move left, in the negative direction, or right, in the positive direction? left

$3 + (-3) =$ 0

2. $-9 + 4$

Where should you start on the number line? −9

Should you move left or right? right

Is the direction you move positive or negative? positive

$-9 + 4 =$ −5

ESSENTIAL QUESTION CHECK-IN

3. Describe how to model the sum $-5 + 4$.

Sample answer: Start at −5. Move to the right 4 units to −1.

Independent Practice

Find each sum.

4. $-8 + 2$ −6
5. $3 + (-9)$ −6
6. $10 + (-7)$ 3
7. $-7 + 7$ 0
8. $-4 + 5$ 1
9. $-11 + 8$ −3

10. During two plays at a football game, the Hawks had a gain of +10 yards followed by a loss of −3 yards. Did they have a total gain or loss of yardage at the end of the two plays? How many yards were gained or lost?

$10 + (-3) = 7$; a gain of 7 yards

11. James deposits $25 in his checking account. After deducting money from an ATM, he writes −$20 in his check register. Which expression best represents the transaction?

A −$25 + $20 B −$25 + (−$20) **(C)** $25 + (−$20) D $25 + $20

12. A submarine at a depth of −50 feet rises 10 feet. What is the depth of the submarine after it rises?

$-50 + 10 = -40$; −40 feet

Elaborate

Talk About It Summarize the Lesson

Ask: How do you use a number line to model addition of integers with different signs? Start at the first integer. Move the number of units indicated by the second integer. Move to the right if the sign of the second integer is positive. Move to the left if the sign of the second integer is negative.

GUIDED PRACTICE Avoid Common Errors

Exercises 1–2 As students write problems with negative numbers, a leading negative sign, as in $-5 + 4$, may get lost. Encourage students to make their negative signs clear and long enough to be seen.

Connect to Daily Life **Mathematical Processes and Practices**

Make sure students understand how negative integers may be used in real-world situations. Examples: a football game where a loss of 3 yards is expressed as −3 yards, a bank account where a withdrawal of 5 dollars is expressed as −5 dollars, a depth where a distance below sea level is expressed as a negative number.

Evaluate

LESSON QUIZ

Find each sum.

1. $-8 + 7$ −1
2. $10 + (-5)$ 5
3. $2 + (-2)$ 0
4. $-9 + 2$ −7
5. $-3 + 12$ 9

H.O.T. FOCUS ON HIGHER ORDER THINKING

1. **Draw Conclusions** You have modeled the sum of 1 plus 3 by starting at 1 on the number line and moving to the right 3 units. Would it be possible to model this by starting at 0? How would this change the instructions? Yes; Sample answer: start at 0, move to 1, and then move 3 units more to the right. **DOK 3; MP.4**

2. **Communicate Mathematical Ideas** For $-7 + 4$, do you need to put parentheses around the −7 or around the 4? Explain. No, Sample answer: the parentheses are needed to separate two operation signs, such as + and −. **DOK 3; MP.7**

3. **Represent Real-World Problems** Write an expression that models the movement of a fish that dives 3 feet down and then comes up 2 feet? $-3 + 2$ **DOK 2; MP.4**

4. **Communicate Mathematical Ideas** Explain how 12 and −12 are the same. How are they different? They are the same number of units away from zero. The difference is 12 is 12 units to the right of 0, while −12 is 12 units to the left of 0. **DOK 3; MP.2**

GETTING READY FOR GRADE 7

GR1.3 Model Integer Multiplication

Engage

ESSENTIAL QUESTION

How can you use a number line to model multiplication of integers with different signs? When multiplying a negative number by a positive number, the positive number tells how many groups to move. The negative number tells how many units to move left each time.

Motivate the Lesson

Ask: How can you use repeated addition and skip counting ideas to model multiplication of integers with different signs on a number line? Begin the Explore Activity to find out.

Explore

EXPLORE ACTIVITY Avoid Common Errors

Some students may not know the mathematical meaning of two parentheses written together, such as in (3)(−5). Remind them this is the same as (3) × (−5) or (3) · (−5).

Focus on Reasoning **Mathematical Processes and Practices**

For A, ask students if the number line graph would be different for (−4)(1). Discuss how the same graph would show both (−4)(1) and (1)(−4) since the negative number tells how many units to move left each time.

Explain

YOUR TURN Avoid Common Errors

Some students may forget which way to move on the number line for a negative number. Remind these students left represents a negative move and right represents a positive move.

GETTING READY FOR GRADE 7

LESSON GR1.3 **Model Integer Multiplication**

ESSENTIAL QUESTION

How can you use a number line to model multiplication of integers?

EXPLORE ACTIVITY

You can think of multiplication as repeated addition or skip counting on a number line.

4(−2) = (−2) + (−2) + (−2) + (−2) or 4 groups of (−2).

To find the product of 4(−2), start at 0. Move 2 units to the left 4 times.

4(−2) = −8

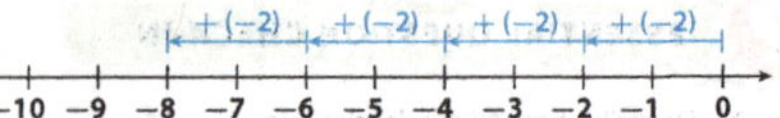

Model each product on a number line.

A (4)(−1)

(4)(−1) = (−1) + (−1) + (−1) + (−1) or 4 groups of (−1).

Start at 0 and move 1 unit to the left 4 times.

(4)(−1) = −4

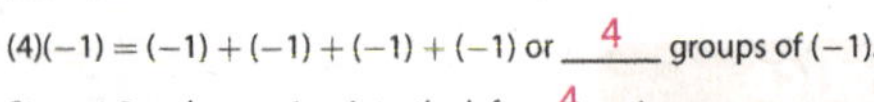

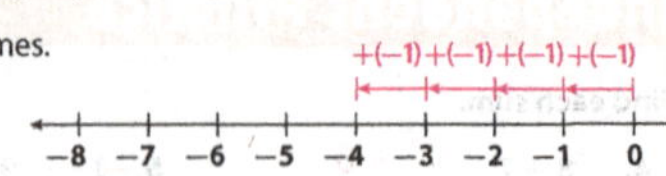

B 2(−3)

2(−3) = (−3) + (−3) or 2 groups of −3.

Start at 0 and move 3 units to the left 2 times.

2(−3) = −6

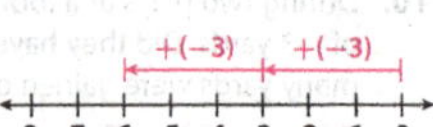

REFLECT

1. Why is the product of a negative integer and a positive integer negative? Because it is like the repeated addition of a negative integer, which has a negative sum.

ADDITIONAL PRACTICE

Find each product.

1. 3(−5) −15 **2.** 2(−3) −6

3. 2(−5) −10 **4.** 1(−2) −2

5. 2(−9) −18 **6.** (3)(−1) −3

7. 4(−3) −12 **8.** 8(−1) −8

9. 4(−5) −20 **10.** 7(−2) −14

YOUR TURN

Use the number line to find each product.

2. (3)(−3) = −9

3. 5(−2) = −10

Guided Practice

Draw a number line to find the product.

1. 5(−4)

Where should you start on the number line? 0

Should you move left or right on the number line? left

Show 5 groups of −4.

5(−4) = −20

2. (6)(−2)

Where should you start on the number line? 0

Is the direction you move positive or negative? negative

Show 6 groups of −2.

(6)(−2) = −12

ESSENTIAL QUESTION CHECK-IN

3. Describe how to use a number line to model the product of 4(−3).

Sample answer: Start at 0. Move 3 units left a total of 4 times.

Independent Practice

Draw a number line to find the product.

4. 2(−8) −16
5. (4)(−7) −28
6. 5(−6) −30
7. 3(−9) −27
8. (9)(−2) −18
9. (8)(−4) −32

10. A diver descended 5 feet from the surface of a lake. She paused and went down another 5 feet. She repeated this one more time. What was the total descent of the diver?

3(−5) = −15; −15 feet

11. The temperature dropped 2 degrees Fahrenheit (°F) every hour over three consecutive hours. By how many degrees Fahrenheit did the temperature change?

3(−2) = −6; −6°F

Elaborate

Talk About It Summarize the Lesson

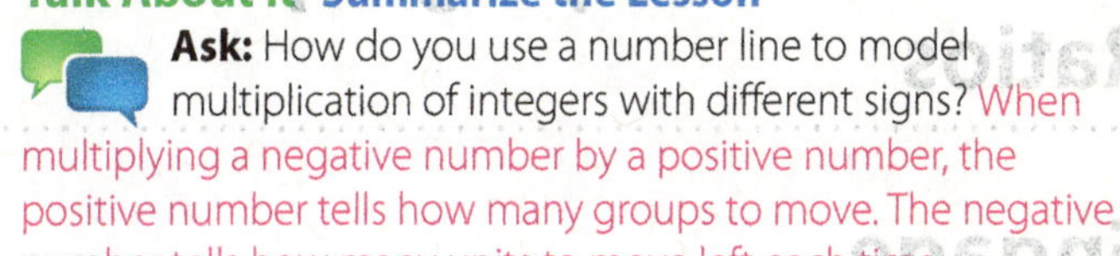

Ask: How do you use a number line to model multiplication of integers with different signs? When multiplying a negative number by a positive number, the positive number tells how many groups to move. The negative number tells how many units to move left each time.

GUIDED PRACTICE Questioning Strategies

- What tells you whether to move to the left or to the right from zero? the negative sign
- What tells you how many groups to move? the positive factor

Avoid Common Errors

Some students may forget to count the initial move from zero to the left as one of the groups. Encourage them to use the number line graph and count each move starting from zero.

Connect to Daily Life **Mathematical Processes and Practices**

Discuss how negative integers are used in daily life by connecting to a bank withdrawal. Taking $4 out of a bank account on 2 different days can be expressed as 2(−4). Similarly, connect to a football game, where 3 losses of 2 yards each is expressed by 3(−2).

Evaluate

LESSON QUIZ

Find each product.

1. 8(−7) −56
2. 10(−5) −50
3. 2(−2) −4
4. 9(−3) −27
5. 2(−11) −22

H.O.T. FOCUS ON HIGHER ORDER THINKING

1. **Analyze Relationships** Can you write an expression for the product of −7 and 4 without using parentheses? Explain. Yes; −7 × 4. **DOK 2; MP.3**

2. **Analyze Relationships** Can you write an expression for the product of −7 and 4 without using a multiplication sign? Explain. Yes; −7(4) or 4(−7) or (4)(−7) or (−7)(4) **DOK 2; MP.3**

3. **Represent Real-World Problems** The temperature fell 10 degrees every hour from 8 P.M. until 11 P.M. Write an expression to represent how the temperature changed during this time. 3(−10) **DOK 2; MP.4**

4. **Draw Conclusions** Explain how to solve 4 (−3) using repeated addition. Sample answer: Rewrite the problem and add (−3) four times. (−3) +, (−3) + (−3) + (−3) = −12 **DOK 3; MP.7**

GETTING READY FOR GRADE 7

GR2.1 Identifying Equivalent Ratios

Engage

ESSENTIAL QUESTION

How can you find equivalent ratios? Rewrite the ratio either by simplifying it (dividing numerator and denominator by the same number) or by extending it (multiplying numerator and denominator by the same number).

Motivate the Lesson

Ask: If the ratio of blue beads to red beads must be $\frac{5}{3}$, how many blue beads do you need when you have 9 red beads? Begin the Explore Activity to find out.

Explore

EXPLORE ACTIVITY

Avoid Common Errors

Some students may not know the mathematical meaning of *equivalent*. Explain that when the values are equal, the two fractions (or ratios) are *equivalent*, even if their forms may look different. For example, $\frac{3}{4}$ and $\frac{9}{12}$ have the same value, even though they are written differently.

Questioning Strategies

- When are two numbers equivalent? When the two numbers have the same value.
- How can two different ratios be equivalent? When the two ratios have the same value.

Explain

YOUR TURN

Focus on Reasoning

Mathematical Practices

Exercise 1 Help students understand that multiplying by $\frac{2}{2}$ is exactly the same as multiplying by 1. Multiplying a number by 1 (in any form) leaves the value unchanged, even though the number may look different.

GETTING READY FOR GRADE 7

LESSON GR2.1 **Identifying Equivalent Ratios**

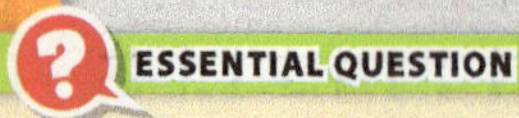

ESSENTIAL QUESTION

How can you find equivalent ratios?

EXPLORE ACTIVITY

Equivalent ratios name the same comparison. Multiply or divide both terms of a ratio by the same number to find equivalent ratios.

$\frac{2}{3} = \frac{2 \times 4}{3 \times 4} = \frac{8}{12}$ $\quad \frac{8}{12} = \frac{8 \div 4}{12 \div 4} = \frac{2}{3}$ $\quad \frac{2}{3}$ and $\frac{8}{12}$ are equivalent ratios.

A The ratio $\frac{5}{3}$ compares the number of blue beads and red beads used to make key chains. Make a table to write equivalent ratios. Multiply both terms of the ratio by the same factor.

		5 × 2 ↓	5 × 3 ↓	5 × 4 ↓
Blue Beads	5	10	15	20
Red Beads	3	6	9	12
		↑ 3 × 2	↑ 3 × 3	↑ 3 × 4

From the table, write the three ratios that are equivalent to $\frac{5}{3}$.

$\frac{10}{6}, \frac{15}{9}, \frac{20}{12}$

B Use division to find ratios equivalent to $\frac{6}{12}$. Divide both terms of the ratio by a common factor. Try 2, 3, and 6. Complete the equations.

2: $\frac{6}{12} = \frac{6 \div 2}{12 \div 2} = \frac{3}{6}$ $\quad$ 3: $\frac{6}{12} = \frac{6 \div 3}{12 \div 3} = \frac{2}{4}$ $\quad$ 6: $\frac{6}{12} = \frac{6 \div 6}{12 \div 6} = \frac{1}{2}$

Write the three ratios you found that are equivalent to $\frac{6}{12}$.

$\frac{3}{6}, \frac{2}{4}, \frac{1}{2}$

YOUR TURN

Write two equivalent ratios for the given ratio. Sample answers are given.

1. $\frac{2}{5}$ $\quad \frac{4}{10}, \frac{6}{15}$ $\qquad$ **2.** $\frac{6}{8}$ $\quad \frac{3}{4}, \frac{12}{16}$ $\qquad$ **3.** $\frac{7}{2}$ $\quad \frac{14}{4}, \frac{21}{6}$

ADDITIONAL PRACTICE

Write two equivalent ratios for the given ratio. Sample answers are given.

1. $\frac{3}{5}$ $\quad \frac{6}{10}, \frac{9}{15}$ $\qquad$ **2.** $\frac{12}{20}$ $\quad \frac{6}{10}, \frac{3}{5}$

3. $\frac{7}{14}$ $\quad \frac{1}{2}, \frac{3}{6}$ $\qquad$ **4.** $\frac{4}{12}$ $\quad \frac{1}{3}, \frac{8}{24}$

5. $\frac{3}{2}$ $\quad \frac{6}{4}, \frac{9}{6}$ $\qquad$ **6.** $\frac{2}{3}$ $\quad \frac{6}{9}, \frac{4}{6}$

7. $\frac{5}{8}$ $\quad \frac{10}{16}, \frac{15}{24}$ $\qquad$ **8.** $\frac{4}{9}$ $\quad \frac{8}{18}, \frac{12}{27}$

Guided Practice

Find the missing terms to make the group of ratios form equivalent ratios.

1. $\frac{5}{8}, \frac{?}{64}, \frac{60}{?}$

Look at $\frac{5}{8}$ and $\frac{?}{64}$ first.

Divide 64 by 8 to find the common factor, 8.

Multiply 5 by the factor to find the missing number: $\frac{?}{64} = \frac{40}{64}$

Look at $\frac{5}{8}$ and $\frac{60}{?}$ next.

Divide 60 by 5 to find the common factor, 12.

Multiply 8 by the factor to find the missing number: $\frac{60}{?} = \frac{60}{96}$

ESSENTIAL QUESTION CHECK-IN

2. How can you use multiplication or division to find equivalent ratios?

Sample answer: Multiply or divide both terms of the ratio by the same number to make an equivalent ratio.

Independent Practice

Find the missing terms to make the group of ratios form equivalent ratios.

3. $\frac{1}{6}, \frac{5}{30}, \frac{8}{48}$
4. $\frac{4}{3}, \frac{28}{21}, \frac{44}{33}$
5. $\frac{3}{8}, \frac{15}{40}, \frac{27}{72}$
6. $\frac{5}{10}, \frac{1}{2}, \frac{35}{70}$
7. $\frac{16}{4}, \frac{8}{2}, \frac{4}{1}$
8. $\frac{2}{8}, \frac{1}{4}, \frac{16}{64}$
9. Which ratio is **not** equivalent to $\frac{6}{8}$?

A $\frac{3}{4}$ **B $\frac{12}{18}$**   C $\frac{18}{24}$ D $\frac{36}{48}$

10. A recipe calls for 18 cups of flour and 12 cups of raisins. Samantha wants to make one-third of the recipe. How many cups of flour and raisins will she need?

6 cups of flour and 4 cups of raisins

Elaborate

Talk About It **Summarize the Lesson**

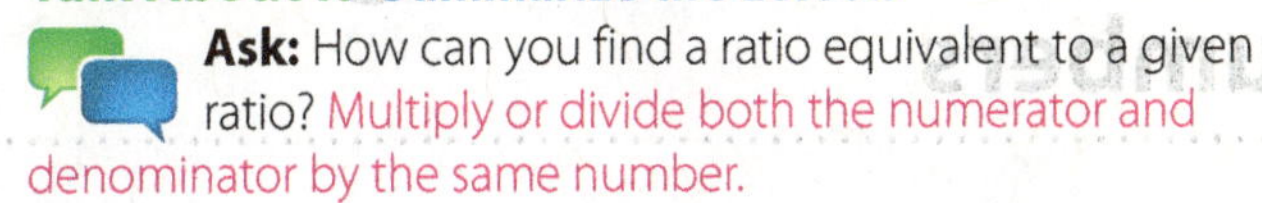

Ask: How can you find a ratio equivalent to a given ratio? Multiply or divide both the numerator and denominator by the same number.

GUIDED PRACTICE **Avoid Common Errors**

Some students try to find equivalent ratios by adding or subtracting the same number from both terms of the ratio. Emphasize that this does not give an equivalent ratio. Discuss the difference between multiplying by 1 (leaves the value unchanged) and adding 1 (changes the value).

Connect to Daily Life **Mathematical Processes and Practices**

Have students discuss how you halve or double a recipe. Point out that every ingredient is multiplied or divided by the same number to create equivalent ratios.

Evaluate

LESSON QUIZ

Find the missing terms to make the group of ratios form equivalent ratios.

1. $\frac{1}{3}, \frac{4}{12}, \frac{5}{15}$
2. $\frac{12}{10}, \frac{36}{30}, \frac{24}{20}$
3. $\frac{12}{16}, \frac{3}{4}, \frac{9}{12}$
4. $\frac{14}{2}, \frac{7}{1}, \frac{21}{3}$

H.O.T. FOCUS ON HIGHER ORDER THINKING

1. **Analyze Relationships** Is the expression $\frac{6}{12}$ equivalent to the expression $\frac{3}{6} \times \frac{2}{2}$? Explain. Yes. To multiply fractions, multiply the numerators by each other and denominators by each other. So $\frac{3}{6} \times \frac{2}{2} = \frac{3 \times 2}{6 \times 2}$, which is $\frac{6}{12}$. **DOK 3; MP.3**

2. **Draw Conclusions** How many ratios could you write that would be equivalent to $\frac{2}{3}$? Explain. There is not a limit; you can always multiply the numerator and denominator by another number. **DOK 3; MP.3**

3. **Analyze Relationships** Is the ratio $\frac{3}{5}$ equivalent to the ratio $\frac{3+4}{5+4}$? Explain. No, adding or subtracting the same number changes the value. **DOK 3; MP.7**

4. **Represent Real-World Problems** A recipe calls for 12 cups of flour and 4 cups of milk. Dave wants to use just 3 cups of flour. What factor should he use to multiply or divide the cups of milk? How many cups of milk should he use? Explain. Since $\frac{12}{4} = \frac{3}{1}$ he should divide the numerator and denominator by 4. He should use 1 cup of milk. **DOK 3; MP.1**

GETTING READY FOR GRADE 7

GR2.2 Model Adding Rational Numbers

Engage

ESSENTIAL QUESTION

How can you model adding rational numbers with different signs?

Model adding rational numbers with different signs by using a number line. Start with the first addend and move right if the second addend is positive and move left if it is negative.

Motivate the Lesson

Ask: How can a number line be used to show addition of rational numbers? Begin the Explore Activity to find out.

Explore

EXPLORE ACTIVITY Avoid Common Errors

Remind students that the first addend tells you the starting point, and the sign of the second addend tells which way to move from there.

Explore

YOUR TURN Avoid Common Errors

Some students may not locate correctly numbers such as $\frac{1}{3}$ or $\frac{5}{6}$ or –6.5 on a number line. Suggest that they divide the unit distance into the same number of parts as the largest denominator (with fractions) or into ten parts (with decimal numbers).

Talk About It Check for Understanding

Ask: When you add or subtract fractions, what must be true about both denominators? What is the process for adding fractions?

Sample answer: The fractions must have a common denominator; add the numerators and use the common denominator for the sum.

GETTING READY FOR GRADE 7

LESSON GR2.2 **Model Adding Rational Numbers**

ESSENTIAL QUESTION

How can you model adding rational numbers with different signs?

EXPLORE ACTIVITY

Use a number line to add rational numbers. Start at the first addend. Move to the right if the number you are adding is positive and to the left if the number is negative.

Model each sum on a number line.

A $-1\frac{3}{4} + \left(-\frac{3}{4}\right)$

Start at $-1\frac{3}{4}$. To move in the negative direction, move left.

Each unit on the number line is $\frac{1}{4}$. To add $-\frac{3}{4}$, move 3 units to the left.

$-1\frac{3}{4} + \left(-\frac{3}{4}\right) = -2\frac{2}{4}$ or $-2\frac{1}{2}$

B $-2.5 + 4.5$

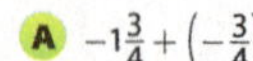

Start at –2.5. To move in the positive direction, move right.

Each unit on the number line is 1. To add 4.5, move 4.5 units right.

$-2.5 + 4.5 =$ 2

REFLECT

1. How is adding rational numbers different from adding integers on a number line?

Adding rational numbers is different because you may have to move a fraction of a unit, instead of a whole unit, to add rational numbers.

YOUR TURN

Use the number line to find each sum.

2. $-2\frac{5}{6} + \left(-\frac{5}{6}\right)$ $-3\frac{4}{6}$ or $-3\frac{2}{3}$

3. $(-6.5) + 2$ -4.5

Getting Ready Lesson 2.2 18

ADDITIONAL PRACTICE

Find each sum. Sketch a number line as a model to help as needed.

1. $2\frac{1}{2} + \left(-1\frac{1}{2}\right)$ 1
2. $1\frac{1}{4} + \left(-2\frac{1}{2}\right)$ $-1\frac{1}{4}$
3. $-1\frac{1}{3} + \left(-4\frac{1}{6}\right)$ $-5\frac{1}{2}$
4. $-3\frac{1}{2} + \left(-2\frac{3}{4}\right)$ $-6\frac{1}{4}$
5. $-4\frac{5}{6} + 2\frac{1}{3}$ $-2\frac{1}{2}$
6. $4.3 + (-2.3)$ 2
7. $-9.6 + 2.6$ -7
8. $-5.2 + (-6.3)$ -11.5
9. $5.4 + (-3)$ 2.4
10. $-9.2 + (-2.9)$ -12.1

Guided Practice

Model the sum on the number line.

1. $-4\frac{1}{4} + 1\frac{2}{4}$

Where should you start on the number line? $-4\frac{1}{4}$

Should you move left or right? right

Is the direction you move positive or negative? positive

What number are you adding to $-4\frac{1}{4}$? $1\frac{2}{4}$

How can you count the units on the number line?

Change $1\frac{2}{4}$ to $\frac{6}{4}$ and count 6 units right.

$-4\frac{1}{4} + 1\frac{2}{4} =$ $-2\frac{3}{4}$

ESSENTIAL QUESTION CHECK-IN

2. How can you determine the sign of the sum when you add two rational numbers?

Sample answer: The addend that lies farthest from 0 on the number line will be the sign of the sum.

Independent Practice

Use a number line to find each sum.

3. $-1\frac{1}{3} + \left(-4\frac{1}{3}\right)$ $-5\frac{2}{3}$

4. $2\frac{2}{4} + \left(-5\frac{3}{4}\right)$ $-3\frac{1}{4}$

5. $-2\frac{1}{6} + 4\frac{5}{6}$ $2\frac{4}{6}$ or $2\frac{2}{3}$

6. $9.5 + (-3.5)$ 6

7. $-2.5 + (-6)$ -8.5

8. $-11.5 + 4.5$ -7

9. Paula makes punch using $1\frac{1}{2}$ cups of orange juice, $2\frac{3}{4}$ cups of lemonade, and $4\frac{3}{4}$ cups of sparkling water. How many cups of punch does Paula make?

9 cups

10. Find each of the following sums of a rational number and its opposite. Then answer the question.

A $-5\frac{2}{3} + 5\frac{2}{3}$ B $1\frac{3}{4} + \left(-1\frac{3}{4}\right)$ C $3.5 + (-3.5)$ D $-7.25 + 7.25$

What is the sum when you add a rational number and its opposite? 0

Elaborate

Talk About It Summarize the Lesson

Ask: How can you tell what sign the sum of two rational numbers will have? Sample answer: If the signs of the addends are the same, the sum will have the same sign. If the signs of the addends are different, the sum will have the sign of the addend that is farthest from zero on a number line.

GUIDED PRACTICE Engage with the Whiteboard

Have students draw and describe the following on a number line: a) both ends of a number line, b) how units are marked and labeled, c) the starting point, d) the direction and length of the move, and e) the answer.

Avoid Common Errors

Exercises 3–8 Remind students that the second addend determines which direction to move on the number line.

Evaluate

LESSON QUIZ

Find each sum. Sketch a number line as a model to help as needed.

1. $-3.8 + 5.1$ 1.3
2. $3\frac{3}{4} + \left(-2\frac{1}{4}\right)$ $1\frac{1}{2}$
3. $-4.6 + (-2.4)$ -7
4. $3\frac{1}{3} + \left(-5\frac{5}{6}\right)$ $-2\frac{1}{2}$

H.O.T. FOCUS ON HIGHER ORDER THINKING

1. **Analyze Relationships** What rational number would you add to $-3\frac{3}{4}$ to get a sum of zero? Explain. $3\frac{3}{4}$; the sum of a rational number and its opposite is always zero. **DOK 3; MP.7**

2. **Communicate Mathematical Ideas** What is the same and what is different about the two rational numbers $-2\frac{5}{6}$ and $2\frac{5}{6}$? Which is the greater number? Explain. They are alike because their distance from zero on a number line is the same. They are different because one is to the right of zero and the other is the left. The greater number is $2\frac{5}{6}$, because it is to the right of $-2\frac{5}{6}$. **DOK 3; MP.3**

3. **Communicate Mathematical Ideas** Compare adding rational numbers on a number line with adding integers on a number line. What is the same and what is different? The steps are the same, but the units on a number line will need to be divided into smaller parts when adding rational numbers. **DOK 3; MP.3**

4. **Analyze Relationships** Which has the greater sum, $-1\frac{1}{4} + 3\frac{3}{4}$ or $3\frac{3}{4} + \left(-1\frac{1}{4}\right)$? If you model each sum on a number line, will the models be the same or different? Explain. The sums are the same; The starting points are different and the models will look different, but the sums are the same. **DOK 3; MP.3**

GETTING READY FOR GRADE 7

GR2.3 Model Subtracting Rational Numbers

Engage

ESSENTIAL QUESTION

How can you change subtracting rational numbers into adding rational numbers? Since subtracting means adding the opposite, rewrite subtracting the second number as adding the opposite of the second number.

Motivate the Lesson

Ask: How can you model subtraction problems on a number line to find their solutions? Begin the Explore Activity to find out.

Explore

EXPLORE ACTIVITY

Focus on Modeling **Mathematical Processes and Practices**

Show students that when you model, on a number line, subtracting a positive number, like $-5 - 2$, will have the same model as adding a negative number, like $-5 + (-2)$. Both expressions have a difference of -7.

Explain

YOUR TURN **Avoid Common Errors**

Students may want to rewrite the expression $5 - 2$ incorrectly as $2 - 5$. Remind students that the Commutative Property does not apply to subtraction.

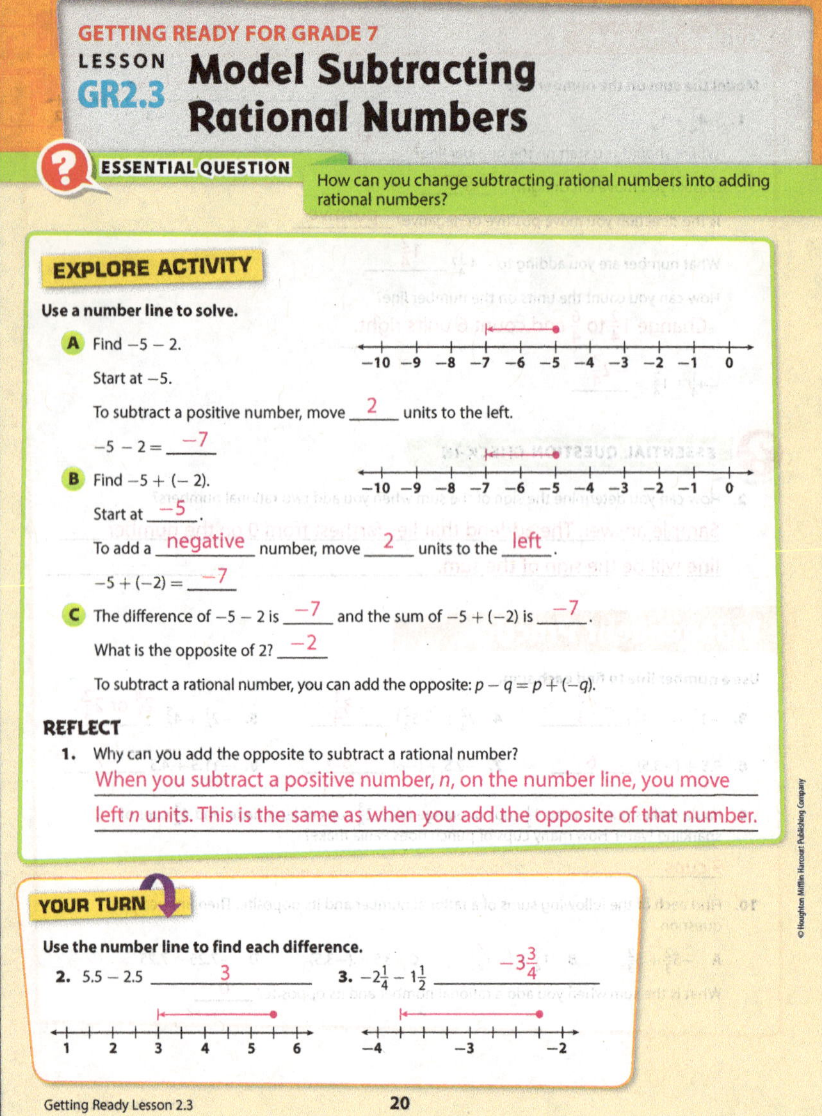

GETTING READY FOR GRADE 7

LESSON GR2.3 **Model Subtracting Rational Numbers**

ESSENTIAL QUESTION

How can you change subtracting rational numbers into adding rational numbers?

EXPLORE ACTIVITY

Use a number line to solve.

A Find $-5 - 2$.

Start at -5.

To subtract a positive number, move 2 units to the left.

$-5 - 2 = -7$

B Find $-5 + (-2)$.

Start at -5.

To add a negative number, move 2 units to the left.

$-5 + (-2) = -7$

C The difference of $-5 - 2$ is -7 and the sum of $-5 + (-2)$ is -7.

What is the opposite of 2? -2

To subtract a rational number, you can add the opposite: $p - q = p + (-q)$.

REFLECT

1. Why can you add the opposite to subtract a rational number? When you subtract a positive number, n, on the number line, you move left n units. This is the same as when you add the opposite of that number.

YOUR TURN

Use the number line to find each difference.

2. $5.5 - 2.5$ 3

3. $-2\frac{1}{4} - 1\frac{1}{2}$ $-3\frac{3}{4}$

Getting Ready Lesson 2.3 20

ADDITIONAL PRACTICE

Rewrite each subtraction as an addition. Then find each sum.

1. $6 - 4$ $6 + (-4); 2$
2. $3 - 8$ $3 + (-8); -5$
3. $-5 - 3$ $-5 + (-3); -8$
4. $11 - 7$ $11 + (-7); 4$
5. $-10 - 10$ $-10 + (-10); -20$
6. $1 - 1$ $1 + (-1); 0$
7. $9 - 6$ $9 + (-6); 3$
8. $-3 - 4$ $-3 + (-4); -7$
9. $12 - 10$ $12 + (-10); 2$
10. $-8 - 2$ $-8 + (-2); -10$

Guided Practice

Use a number line to find each difference or sum.

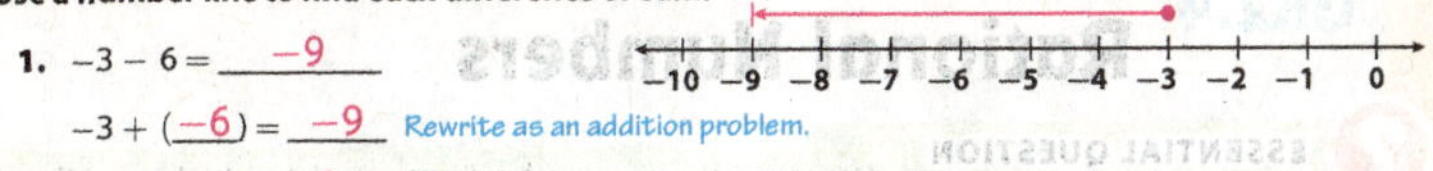

1. $-3-6=$ -9

$-3+(-6)=-9$ Rewrite as an addition problem.

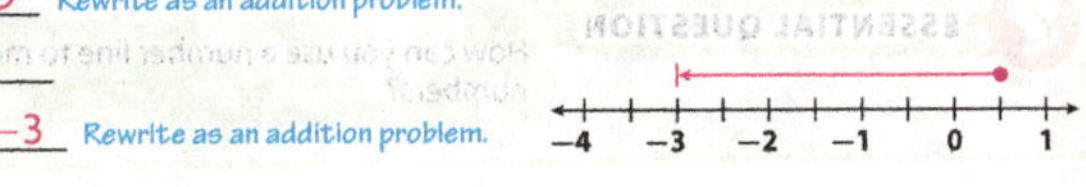

2. $0.5-3.5=-3$

$0.5+(-3.5)=-3$ Rewrite as an addition problem.

ESSENTIAL QUESTION CHECK-IN

3. How can you subtract a rational number by changing the operation to addition?

Sample answer: Change the number being subtracted to its opposite. Then add to the number being subtracted from.

Independent Practice

Use a number line to find each difference. Then, rewrite each as a sum.

4. $-1-6=-7$

$-1+(-6)=-7$

5. $8-12=-4$

$8+(-12)=-4$

6. $-2\frac{1}{6}-4\frac{2}{3}=-6\frac{5}{6}$

$-2\frac{1}{6}+-4\frac{2}{3}=-6\frac{5}{6}$

7. $-2.5-6=-8.5$

$-2.5+(-6)=-8.5$

8. $-9-3=-12$

$-9+(-3)=-12$

9. $12-4=8$

$12+(-4)=8$

10. When Sanjay goes to bed, the temperature is −6 °F. When he wakes up in the morning, the temperature has dropped another 8 °F. What is the temperature when Sanjay wakes up?

−14°F

11. Mariana withdraws \$20 from her bank account. Later she writes a check for \$15.

Which amount represents the total change to her bank account?

A −\$35 (circled) **B** −\$5 **C** \$5 **D** \$35

12. How are the expressions $-4-4$ and $-4+(-4)$ the same? How are they different?

Sample answer: Both expressions are equal to the same number: −8. One expression subtracts a positive 4 and the other adds a negative 4.

Elaborate

Talk About It **Summarize the Lesson**

Ask: How is subtracting rational numbers similar to adding rational numbers? Subtraction of rational numbers can be rewritten as addition of the opposite.

GUIDED PRACTICE Engage with the Whiteboard

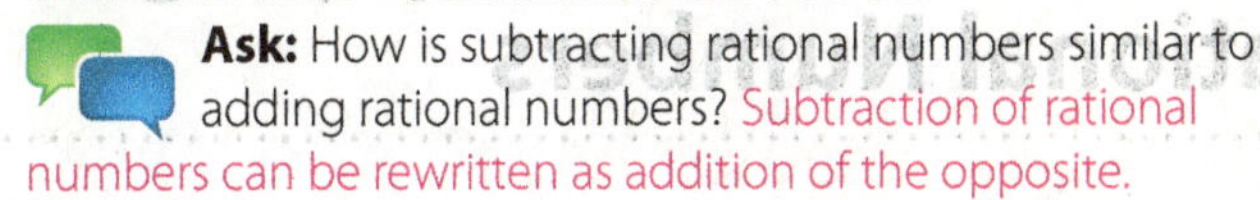

Have students model the expression $-2\frac{1}{2}-\left(7\frac{1}{2}\right)$. Then have the students model the expression $-2\frac{1}{2}+\left(-7\frac{1}{2}\right)$. Have the students compare the models and the sums and differences.

Connect Vocabulary ELL

In subtraction, the minuend is the number from which we subtract and the number we are subtracting is called the subtrahend. Notice they have different names, reminding us that subtraction is not commutative.

Evaluate

LESSON QUIZ

Find each sum. Sketch a number line as a model to help as needed.

1. $5.1-3.6$ 1.5
2. $3\frac{1}{2}-2\frac{1}{4}$ $1\frac{1}{4}$
3. $-4.5-2.3$ −6.8
4. $3\frac{1}{3}-5\frac{1}{2}$ $-2\frac{1}{6}$

H.O.T. FOCUS ON HIGHER ORDER THINKING

1. **Multiple Representations** If you walked on a number line from −5 to 3, which direction would you be walking? How many units would your walk be? How might you represent this mathematically? You would be walking to the right for 8 units; $-5+8=3$ **DOK 2; MP.3**

2. **Analyze Relationships** On a number line, how many units is −11 from zero? How many units is 8 from zero? Which is farther from zero? Which is the greater number? −11 is 11 units from zero; 8 is 8 units from zero. −11 is farther from zero. 8 is the greater number. **DOK 3; MP.3**

3. **Draw Conclusions** Is $-6+(4)$ the same as $4+(-6)$? Explain. Yes; Addition is commutative and subtraction is not. So, you can change the order when adding, but not when subtracting. **DOK 3; MP.7**

4. **Communicate Mathematical Ideas** Can you rewrite $9+(-5)$ as $9-5$? Explain. Since subtracting is the same as adding the opposite, $9-5=9+(-5)$. **DOK 3; MP.3**

GETTING READY FOR GRADE 7

GR2.4 Model Multiplying Rational Numbers

Engage

ESSENTIAL QUESTION

How can you use a number line to model multiplying rational numbers? When multiplying a negative number by a positive number, the positive number tells how many groups to move. The negative number tells how many spaces to move left each time.

Motivate the Lesson

Ask: How is multiplying with rational numbers different than multiplying with whole numbers? How can you represent multiplication with rational numbers on a number line? Begin the Explore Activity to find out.

Explore

EXPLORE ACTIVITY Engage with the Whiteboard

Have students work in groups to draw 2 groups of −2.5 on a number line. Have students work out the problem on the number line and check their sign using the products with different signs chart.

Explain

YOUR TURN

Questioning Strategies **Mathematical Processes and Practices**

- Which way on the number line represents negative? left
- What are the steps to multiplying 2(−6) on a number line? Start at 0. Show 2 groups of −6. The product is −12.

GETTING READY FOR GRADE 7

LESSON GR2.4 **Model Multiplying Rational Numbers**

ESSENTIAL QUESTION

How can you use a number line to model multiplying rational numbers?

Products with Different Signs		
Factor	Factor	Product
+	−	−
−	+	−

Products with the Same Sign		
Factor	Factor	Product
+	+	+
−	−	+

EXPLORE ACTIVITY

Use a number line to find each product.

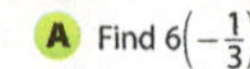

A Find $6\left(-\frac{1}{3}\right)$.

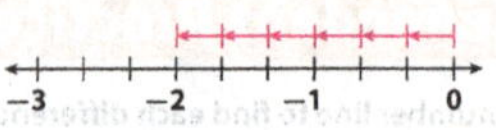

Write as repeated addition.

$6\left(-\frac{1}{3}\right) = \left(-\frac{1}{3}\right) + \left(-\frac{1}{3}\right) + \left(-\frac{1}{3}\right) + \left(-\frac{1}{3}\right) + \left(-\frac{1}{3}\right) + \left(-\frac{1}{3}\right)$

Notice that each unit on the number line is $\frac{1}{3}$. So start at 0 and move 1 unit to the left 6 times.

Use the rules to check the sign of the product: (+)(−) = (−).

$6\left(-\frac{1}{3}\right) =$ −2

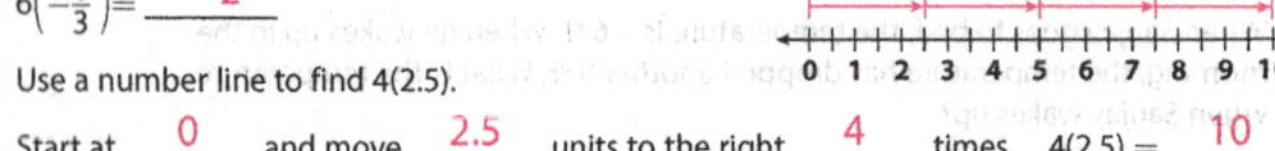

B Use a number line to find 4(2.5).

Start at 0 and move 2.5 units to the right 4 times. 4(2.5) = 10

Use the rules to find the sign of the product: (−)(−) = (+).

−4(−2.5) = 10

REFLECT

1. How does using the chart with the rules for multiplying rational numbers help you multiply rational numbers?

Sample answer: I can find the sign of the product using the chart. Then, I can move left or right on the number line depending on whether the product is positive or negative.

Getting Ready Lesson 2.4 22

ADDITIONAL PRACTICE

Find each product.

1. 4(−1) −4
2. 2(−3) −6
3. 2(−5) −10
4. 1(2) 2
5. 2(9) 18
6. (3)(−1) −3
7. (−3)(−3) 9
8. −8(−1) 8
9. 4(−5) −20
10. 7(−2) −14

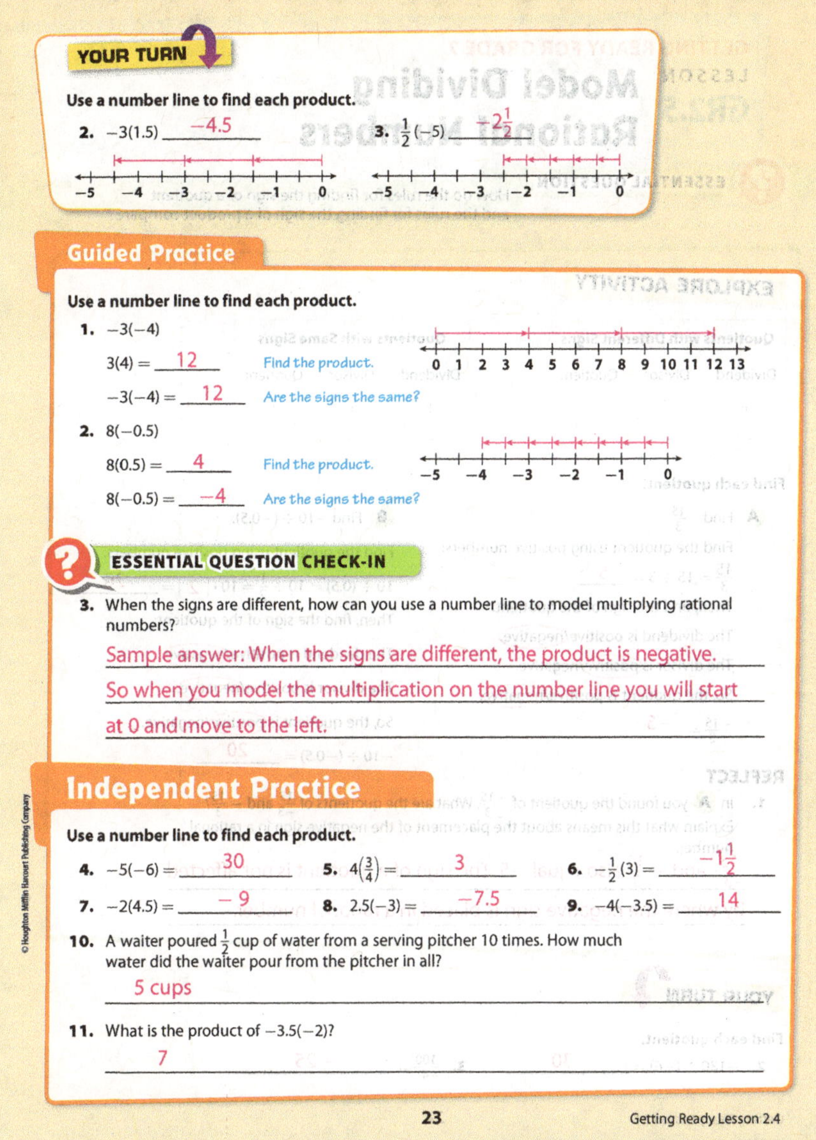

YOUR TURN

Use a number line to find each product.

2. $-3(1.5)$ = -4.5 3. $\frac{1}{2}(-5)$ = $-2\frac{1}{2}$

Guided Practice

Use a number line to find each product.

1. $-3(-4)$

$3(4) =$ 12 Find the product.

$-3(-4) =$ 12 Are the signs the same?

2. $8(-0.5)$

$8(0.5) =$ 4 Find the product.

$8(-0.5) =$ -4 Are the signs the same?

ESSENTIAL QUESTION CHECK-IN

3. When the signs are different, how can you use a number line to model multiplying rational numbers?

Sample answer: When the signs are different, the product is negative. So when you model the multiplication on the number line you will start at 0 and move to the left.

Independent Practice

Use a number line to find each product.

4. $-5(-6) =$ 30 5. $4\left(\frac{3}{4}\right) =$ 3 6. $-\frac{1}{2}(3) =$ $-1\frac{1}{2}$

7. $-2(4.5) =$ -9 8. $2.5(-3) =$ -7.5 9. $-4(-3.5) =$ 14

10. A waiter poured $\frac{1}{2}$ cup of water from a serving pitcher 10 times. How much water did the waiter pour from the pitcher in all?

5 cups

11. What is the product of $-3.5(-2)$?

7

23 Getting Ready Lesson 2.4

Elaborate

Talk About It Summarize the Lesson

Ask: What are the rules for the signs of products when you are multiplying rational numbers? The product will be negative if the two factors have different signs; the product will be positive if the two factors have the same sign.

GUIDED PRACTICE Questioning Strategies

- How do you know to move left or right from zero when multiplying rational numbers on a number line? If the signs of the factors are different, move left. If the signs of the factors are the same, move right.
- How do you know how many groups to move when multiplying rational numbers on a number line? the second factor

Avoid Common Errors

Exercise 1 Some students may forget to count the initial move from zero as one of the groups. Encourage them to use the number line graph and to count each move starting from zero.

Connect to Daily Life Mathematical Processes and Practices

Have students give examples in daily life that could be represented by negative rational numbers, such as debt, falling temperature, diving below sea level, and spending from a bank account.

Evaluate

LESSON QUIZ

Find each product.

1. $8(-1.5)$ -12
2. $\frac{2}{3}(-6)$ -4
3. $-2\left(-\frac{3}{4}\right)$ $1\frac{1}{2}$
4. $9\left(\frac{1}{6}\right)$ $1\frac{1}{2}$

H.O.T. FOCUS ON HIGHER ORDER THINKING

1. **Analyze Relationships** Name two rational numbers that have a product of 2 and a sum of $-4\frac{1}{2}$. $-\frac{1}{2}$ and -4 **DOK 2; MP.2**

2. **Look for a Pattern** What will be the sign of this product? Explain. $-2(13)(-7.8)(102)(-45.3)$ The product will have a negative sign. Since multiplication can be commuted and associated, rearrange in groups of two factors. $[(-2)(-7.8)]\ [(-45.3)(13)]\ (102)$. The product of the first group is positive; the product of the second group is negative, so the product of those together is a negative final product. **DOK 3; MP.7**

2. **Analyze Relationships** Name two integers whose product is -24 and whose sum is 2. 6 and -4 **DOK 2; MP.2**

4. **Look for a Pattern** If you are multiplying with a negative factor and get a positive product, what do you know about the second factor? Explain. The second factor must be negative. In order to get a positive product from a negative factor, both factors must be negative. **DOK 3; MP.7**

GETTING READY FOR GRADE 7

GR2.5 Model Dividing Rational Numbers

Engage

ESSENTIAL QUESTION

How do the rules for finding the sign of a quotient and the rules for finding the sign of a product compare? The rules for products and quotients of signed numbers are alike because of the inverse relationship between multiplication and division. When the signs of the numbers are the same, the result is positive. When the signs are different, the result is negative.

Motivate the Lesson

Ask: Are the rules for dividing rational numbers and dividing integers different or the same? Begin the Explore Activity to find out.

Explore

EXPLORE ACTIVITY Avoid Common Errors

Some students may have trouble relating the fraction form of a division problem to the other forms: $\frac{15}{3} \rightarrow 3\overline{)15} \rightarrow 15 \div 3$. Have them practice writing problems in all three forms, and then ask them to invent their own ways of remembering which number goes on top, in front, or inside $\overline{)\quad}$.

Explain

YOUR TURN

Questioning Strategies Mathematical Processes and Practices

- Why is the answer in exercise 2 positive? The dividend and the divisor have the same signs, so the quotient is positive.
- Why is the answer in exercise 3 negative? The dividend and the divisor have opposite signs, so the quotient is negative.

GETTING READY FOR GRADE 7

LESSON GR2.5 **Model Dividing Rational Numbers**

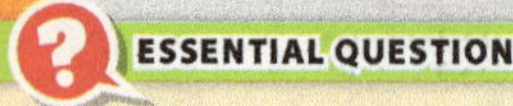

ESSENTIAL QUESTION

How do the rules for finding the sign of a quotient and the rules for finding the sign of a product compare?

EXPLORE ACTIVITY

Quotients with Different Signs

Dividend	Divisor	Quotient
+	−	−
−	+	−

Quotients with Same Signs

Dividend	Divisor	Quotient
+	+	+
−	−	+

Find each quotient.

A Find $-\frac{15}{3}$.

Find the quotient using positive numbers:

$\frac{15}{3} = 15 \div 3 =$ 5

Then, find the sign of the quotient:

The dividend is positive/(negative).

The divisor is (positive)/negative.

So, the quotient is positive/(negative).

$-\frac{15}{3} =$ −5

B Find $-10 \div (-0.5)$.

Find the quotient using positive numbers:

$10 \div (0.5) = 10 \div \frac{1}{2} = 10 \cdot$ [2] $=$ 20

Then, find the sign of the quotient:

The dividend is positive/(negative).

The divisor is positive/(negative).

So, the quotient is (positive)/negative.

$-10 \div (-0.5) =$ 20

REFLECT

1. In **A** you found the quotient of $-\frac{15}{3}$. What are the quotients of $\frac{15}{-3}$ and $-\frac{15}{3}$? Explain what this means about the placement of the negative sign in a rational number.

$\frac{15}{-3}$ and $-\frac{15}{3}$ also equal −5. The sign of a quotient is not affected by where the negative sign is placed in a rational number.

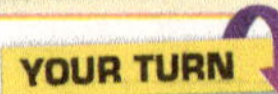

YOUR TURN

Find each quotient.

2. $-180 \div (-6) =$ 30

3. $\frac{100}{-4} =$ −25

ADDITIONAL PRACTICE

Find each quotient.

1. $\frac{35}{5}$ 7
2. $-4\overline{)16}$ −4
3. $44 \div 11$ 4
4. $\frac{-20}{2}$ −10
5. $\frac{16}{-0.5}$ −32
6. $-100 \div 20$ −5
7. $\frac{-42}{-7}$ 6
8. $-\frac{60}{4}$ −15
9. $32 \div (-8)$ −4
10. $2.8 \div 2$ 1.4

Guided Practice

Find each quotient.

1. $\frac{-36}{9}$

Find the quotient using positive numbers: $36 \div 9 =$ 4

According to the rules, the quotient is positive/negative. (negative circled)

$\frac{-36}{9} =$ −4

2. $-60 \div (-12)$

Find the quotient using positive numbers: $60 \div 12 =$ 5

According to the rules, the quotient is positive/negative. (positive circled)

$-60 \div (-12) =$ 5

ESSENTIAL QUESTION CHECK-IN

3. How are the rules for dividing rational numbers similar to the rules for multiplying rational numbers?

Sample answer: When the signs of both factors or both the dividend and divisor are the same, the answer is positive. When the signs are different, the answer is negative.

Independent Practice

Find each quotient.

4. $-1.2 \div 3 =$ −0.4
5. $\frac{-72}{-9} =$ 8
6. $\frac{45}{-15} =$ −3
7. $7.5 \div (-3) =$ −2.5
8. $-15 \div (-1.5) =$ 10
9. $\frac{320}{80} =$ 4

10. The price of a stock fell $24 in 3 days. What was the average change in the price each day? How do you know?

The average change was −$8 per day; $\frac{-\$24}{3} = -\$8$

11. Why do $\frac{20}{-5}$ and $\frac{-20}{5}$ have the same quotient? Explain your thinking.

Sample answer: When you divide, they both equal −4. The sign of the quotient is not affected by the placement of the negative sign in the rational number.

Elaborate

Talk About It Summarize the Lesson

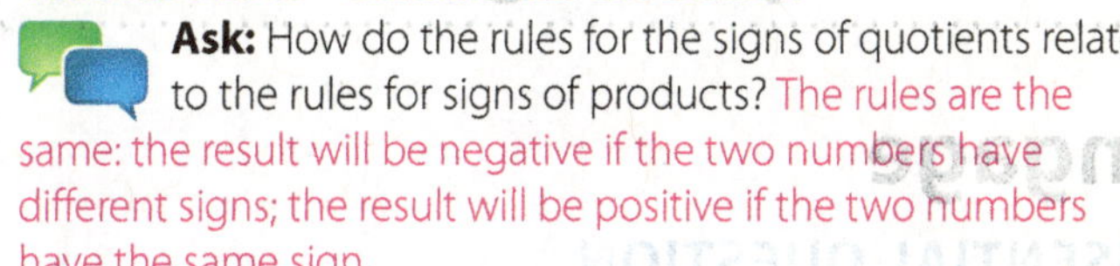

Ask: How do the rules for the signs of quotients relate to the rules for signs of products? The rules are the same: the result will be negative if the two numbers have different signs; the result will be positive if the two numbers have the same sign.

GUIDED PRACTICE

Avoid Common Errors

Exercise 1 Some students may, after finding the quotient using positive numbers, forget to use the appropriate sign for the original problem. Remind them to decide on the sign of the answer FIRST, and write it down, and then to do the calculations. Suggest that they check their work in two parts: first, is the sign correct? and second, is the quotient correct?

Evaluate

LESSON QUIZ

Find each product.

1. $\frac{9}{-0.5}$ −18
2. $68 \div (-2)$ −34
3. $\frac{-32}{-8}$ 4
4. $-10.5 \div 5$ −2.1

H.O.T. FOCUS ON HIGHER ORDER THINKING

1. **Analyze Relationships** Write two equivalent expressions for $-\frac{4}{5}$ using the same digits. $\frac{-4}{5}$, $\frac{4}{-5}$ **DOK 2; MP.3**

2. **Communicate Mathematical Ideas** What does it mean to say that multiplication and division are inverse operations? Explain with examples. Multiplication and division undo each other. The factors in multiplication will be the divisor and quotient in division. For example, $5 \cdot 2 = 10$; therefore $10 \div 2 = 5$ and $10 \div 5 = 2$. Examples will vary. **DOK 3; MP.2**

3. **Communicate Mathematical Ideas** What is the product when you multiply by zero? What is the quotient when you divide by zero? Support your answers with examples. The product of any number multiplied by 0 is 0. Division by zero is undefined. Examples will vary. **DOK 3; MP.7**

4. **Critical Thinking** What is alike about the rules for multiplication and division of rational numbers and what is different? Give examples. Sample answer: The rules about signs are the same, however, multiplication is commutative and division is not. Examples will vary. **DOK 3; MP.7**

GETTING READY FOR GRADE 7

GR3.1 Exploring Rates

Engage

ESSENTIAL QUESTION

How do you find a unit rate? To find a unit rate, write the rate with a denominator of 1 unit by dividing both numerator and denominator by the number in the denominator.

Motivate the Lesson

Ask: When one bag contains 4 apples at a certain price and another contains 6 apples at a different price, how can you find which costs less per apple? Begin the Explore Activity to find out.

Explore

EXPLORE ACTIVITY Connect Vocabulary ELL

The meaning and use of the word *per* may not be clear to some students. Explain that *per* means "for each." Discuss some examples that may be familiar to them such as a car might drive 30 miles for each gallon, or a person might walk 4 miles for each hour.

Avoid Common Errors

Some students may be confused by the meaning of the words *ratio, rate,* and *unit rate*. You may wish to quickly define *ratio* as a comparison of any two numbers or quantities. A *rate* is a special kind of ratio that compares quantities measured in different units, such as miles per hour, or words per minute. A *unit rate* is a special kind of rate where the denominator is 1 unit.

Explain

YOUR TURN Avoid Common Errors

In Your Turn Exercise 2, some students may not understand how to convert 15 minutes to $\frac{1}{4}$ hour. Remind them there are 60 minutes in one hour, so 15 minutes is $\frac{15 \text{ minutes}}{60 \text{ minutes}}$ or $\frac{1}{4}$ hour.

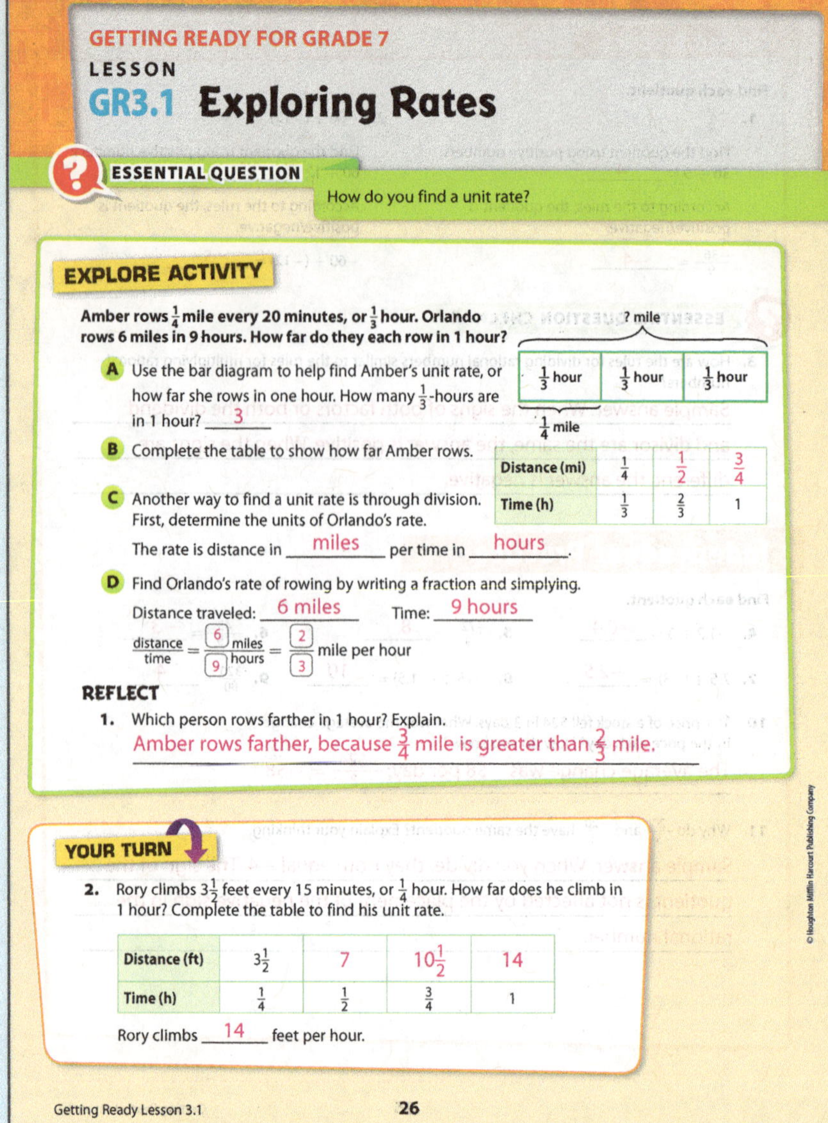
GETTING READY FOR GRADE 7

LESSON

GR3.1 Exploring Rates

ESSENTIAL QUESTION

How do you find a unit rate?

EXPLORE ACTIVITY

Amber rows $\frac{1}{4}$ mile every 20 minutes, or $\frac{1}{3}$ hour. Orlando rows 6 miles in 9 hours. How far do they each row in 1 hour?

A Use the bar diagram to help find Amber's unit rate, or how far she rows in one hour. How many $\frac{1}{3}$-hours are in 1 hour? 3

B Complete the table to show how far Amber rows.

Distance (mi)	$\frac{1}{4}$	$\frac{1}{2}$	$\frac{3}{4}$
Time (h)	$\frac{1}{3}$	$\frac{2}{3}$	1

C Another way to find a unit rate is through division. First, determine the units of Orlando's rate.

The rate is distance in miles per time in hours.

D Find Orlando's rate of rowing by writing a fraction and simplifying.

Distance traveled: 6 miles Time: 9 hours

$\frac{\text{distance}}{\text{time}} = \frac{6 \text{ miles}}{9 \text{ hours}} = \frac{2}{3}$ mile per hour

REFLECT

1. Which person rows farther in 1 hour? Explain.
Amber rows farther, because $\frac{3}{4}$ mile is greater than $\frac{2}{3}$ mile.

YOUR TURN

2. Rory climbs $3\frac{1}{2}$ feet every 15 minutes, or $\frac{1}{4}$ hour. How far does he climb in 1 hour? Complete the table to find his unit rate.

Distance (ft)	$3\frac{1}{2}$	7	$10\frac{1}{2}$	14
Time (h)	$\frac{1}{4}$	$\frac{1}{2}$	$\frac{3}{4}$	1

Rory climbs 14 feet per hour.

Getting Ready Lesson 3.1 26

ADDITIONAL PRACTICE

Find each unit rate.

1. 2 miles every $\frac{1}{2}$ hour 4 miles per hour
2. 4 miles every 6 hours $\frac{2}{3}$ mile per hour
3. $4\frac{1}{2}$ feet every $\frac{1}{3}$ hour $13\frac{1}{2}$ feet per hour
4. 1,000 words in 5 minutes 200 words per minute
5. 7 miles in $\frac{1}{4}$ hour 28 miles per hour
6. $3\frac{1}{2}$ yards in $\frac{1}{3}$ hour $10\frac{1}{2}$ yards per hour
7. 500 gallons in 10 minutes 50 gallons per minute
8. 30 feet in 10 seconds 3 feet per second
9. $3.00 dollars for 5 apples $0.60 per apple
10. $3.75 for 5 used books $0.75 per used book

Guided Practice

Find each unit rate.

1. Joaquin read 2,600 words in 8 minutes.

Identify units: words per minute

Write a fraction: $\frac{2,600 \text{ words}}{8 \text{ minutes}}$

Simplify: $\frac{2,600 \text{ words}}{8 \text{ minutes}} = \frac{325 \text{ words}}{1 \text{ minute}}$

Joaquin read 325 words per minute.

2. Thanh drove 6 miles in $\frac{1}{5}$ hour.

Distance (mi)	6	12	18	24	30
Time (h)	$\frac{1}{5}$	$\frac{2}{5}$	$\frac{3}{5}$	$\frac{4}{5}$	1

Thanh drove 30 miles per hour.

ESSENTIAL QUESTION CHECK-IN

3. Which is better in comparing rates, the rate or the unit rate?

Sample answer: The unit rate because the denominator is the same, which allows you to compare the rates directly.

Independent Practice

Find each unit rate.

4. $2\frac{1}{4}$ yards in $\frac{1}{2}$ hour
$4\frac{1}{2}$ yards per hour

5. $\frac{2}{5}$ m in $\frac{1}{10}$ minute
4 m per minute

6. $\frac{2}{3}$ feet in $\frac{1}{12}$ sec
8 feet per sec

7. $5\frac{1}{2}$ mi in $\frac{1}{4}$ day
22 mi per day

8. A diver descends 50 feet every $\frac{1}{4}$ hour. What is the diver's unit rate?
200 feet per hour

9. You can buy 5 cans of green beans on sale at the Village Market for $3.00. You can buy 10 of the same cans of green beans at Member's Warehouse for $6.70. Which is the better buy? Explain your thinking.
The green beans from the Village Market. Possible answer: The unit price of the green beans from Village Market is $0.60 per can while the unit price from the Member's Warehouse is $0.67 per can. $0.60 is less than $0.67.

Elaborate

Talk About It

Summarize the Lesson

Ask: What is a unit rate and how do you find it? A unit rate is a rate that has 1 unit as the denominator. To write a rate as a unit rate, divide numerator and denominator by the number in the denominator, or use a table to count fractional parts up to 1.

GUIDED PRACTICE

Avoid Common Errors

Exercise 1 Some students may think incorrectly that $\frac{2,600}{8}$ means "8 divided by 2,600." Have them practice writing in several different equivalent division forms: $\frac{2600}{8} \rightarrow 8\overline{)2600} \rightarrow$ $2600 \div 8$ and then ask them to write their own example to show the equivalent forms, including in words.

Evaluate

LESSON QUIZ

Find each unit rate.

1. 5 feet every $\frac{1}{2}$ hour 10 feet per hour
2. $4.50 dollars for 5 grapefruit $0.90 per grapefruit
3. 10 miles every 3 hours $3\frac{1}{3}$ miles per hour
4. 25 feet in 20 seconds 1.25 feet per second

H.O.T. FOCUS ON HIGHER ORDER THINKING

1. **Multiple Representations** In the Explore Activity, Amber's rate is $\frac{1}{4}$ mile every 20 minutes. What is her unit rate per minute? $\frac{1}{80}$ mile per minute. What is her unit rate per hour? $\frac{3}{4}$ mile per hour. Which of these three rates is the fastest? All three are equivalent; they are different ways of writing the same ratio. **DOK 3; MP.3**

2. **Represent Real-World Problems** Kate's dog eats 8 ounces of food every 6 hours. How much food does the dog eat in a 24 hour day? What is its unit rate per hour? 32 ounces per day; $1\frac{1}{3}$ ounces per hour **DOK 2; MP.3**

3. **Represent Real-World Problems** When one bag of 4 apples costs $1.80 and another bag of 6 apples costs $2.10, which is the better buy and what are the different costs per apple? The bag of 6 apples is the better buy; each of these apples costs $0.35 while the 4 apples in the other bag cost $0.45 each. **DOK 3; MP.3**

4. **Look for a Pattern** Use an example to show how could you change a rate of miles per hour to a rate of miles per minute. Sample answer: 45 miles per hour is 45 miles per 60 minutes or $\frac{45 \text{ miles}}{60 \text{ minutes}} = \frac{45 \div 15}{60 \div 15} = \frac{3}{4}$ for a unit rate of $\frac{3}{4}$ mile per minute. **DOK 3; MP.7**

GETTING READY FOR GRADE 7

GR3.2 Constant Rates of Change

Engage

ESSENTIAL QUESTION

How can you tell if a relationship is a proportional relationship? In a proportional relationship, the rate of change is constant between two quantities.

Motivate the Lesson

Ask: At the grocery store, is the larger box of cereal always the better buy? Does the price per ounce go up, go down, or stay the same as the size of the package changes? How can you tell? Begin the Explore Activity to find out.

Explore

EXPLORE ACTIVITY Connect Vocabulary ELL

Make sure that students understand the meaning of the word *constant*. Tell them that it means "the same" or "unchanging," and ask students for possible examples. Ask students to explain the meaning of the abbreviations in the table: h and mi.

Questioning Strategies

- How did you find the values in the table? Justify your answer. I took the ratio that was given for 4 hours and multiplied the hour by the unit rate.
- How far could Delia ride her bike if she rode for 6 hours at the same steady pace? 6 hours × 10.5 miles per hour = 63 miles

Explain

YOUR TURN Avoid Common Errors

Exercise 2 Some students may not read the question correctly or have trouble relating it to the table. Read the table to make sure these students understand the table. 1 ride cost 6 tickets, and so on.

GETTING READY FOR GRADE 7

LESSON GR3.2 **Constant Rates of Change**

ESSENTIAL QUESTION How can you tell if a relationship is a proportional relationship?

EXPLORE ACTIVITY

When the rate of change, or the ratio of one quantity to another, is constant between two quantities, the relationship is a *proportional* relationship.

Delia bikes at a steady pace. It takes her 4 hours to travel 42 miles.

A Use the bar diagram to find how many miles Delia bikes in 1 hour. How did you find the answer?

10.5 miles; divide 42 by 4

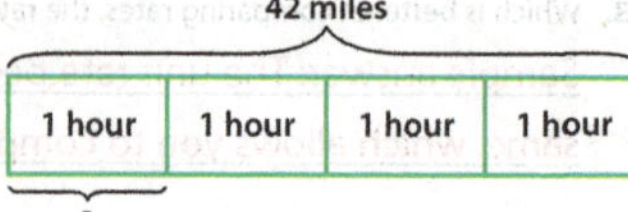

B Complete the table to compare the time and the distance Delia bikes.

Time (h)	1	2	3	4	5
Distance (mi)	10.5	21	31.5	42	52.5

C For each column of the table, write a ratio of the distance to the time. Then write each ratio as a decimal.

$\frac{10.5}{1} = 10.5$ $\frac{21}{2} = 10.5$ $\frac{31.5}{3} = 10.5$ $\frac{42}{4} = 10.5$ $\frac{52.5}{5} = 10.5$

D How do the decimals compare? They are equal.

E Is the relationship between the distance traveled and the time constant or changing? Is it a proportional relationship?

It is constant, so it is a proportional relationship.

REFLECT

1. How can you tell that Delia bikes at a rate that is constant? What is the rate?

Every hour, she bikes the same distance. The rate is 10.5 miles in one hour.

ADDITIONAL PRACTICE

Is the relationship shown in each table a proportional relationship? Explain

1.

Sheep	3	4	5	6
Number of hooves	12	16	20	24

Yes, the rate is constant at 4 hooves per sheep.

2.

Hours worked	6	8	16	20
Dollars earned	72	96	192	240

Yes, the rate is constant at $12 earned per hour.

3.

Height (inches)	18	28	38	48
Time (months)	6	9	12	15

No, the rate is not constant

4.

Time (minutes)	3	5	8	11
Distance (mi)	9	15	24	33

Yes, rate is constant at 3 miles per minute

YOUR TURN

2. Based on the table, is the relationship between the number of tickets purchased and the number of rides a proportional relationship? Explain.

Rides	1	2	3	4
Tickets Purchased	6	12	18	24

Yes, because the rate is constant at 6 tickets per ride.

Guided Practice

1. Roger earns $15 for each lawn he mows.

Number of Lawns	1	2	3	4	5
Amount Earned ($)	15	30	45	60	75

For each column of the table, find the rate.

$15 , $15 , $15 , $15 , $15

Is the relationship between the amount Roger earns and the number of lawns he mows a proportional relationship? Explain.

Yes; Sample answer: The rate is constant; $15 per lawn.

ESSENTIAL QUESTION CHECK-IN

2. How can a table help you determine if a relationship is a proportional relationship?

If the ratios are all equal, then the relationship is proportional.

Independent Practice

3. The table shows the amount that Rajeev earns.

Hours Worked	1	2	3	4	5
Amount Earned ($)	21.50	43	64.5	86	107.50

a. Is the relationship shown in the table proportional? yes

b. Write an equation to represent the relationship, where x is the number of hours worked and y is the amount earned. $y = 21.5x$

c. How much will Rajeev earn if he works for 8 hours? $172

Elaborate

Talk About It Summarize the Lesson

Ask: How can you tell when the relationship between two quantities is a proportional relationship? The relationship is proportional when the ratio of one quantity to the other is constant and does not change.

GUIDED PRACTICE Avoid Common Errors

Exercise 1 Some students may only check the first two rate of change for the first two ratios. Remind students that it is not proportional unless all the pairs have equal rates.

Evaluate

LESSON QUIZ

1. A. Use the relationship in the first column to complete this table so that it shows a proportional relationship.

Bracelets	1	2	3	4	5
Beads	18	36	54	72	90

B. Write an equation to represent the relationship in the table where x is the number of bracelets and y is the number of beads. $y = 18x$

2. Is the relationship shown in this table a proportional one? Explain.

Ounces	10	16	20	45	60
Price	$1.80	$2.60	$3.60	$8.50	$9.00

No, the rates of change are not constant.

H.O.T. FOCUS ON HIGHER ORDER THINKING

1. **Multi-step** The table shows how much Helen can earn, working 6 hours a day, for 1 day up to 5 days, if she is paid $7 an hour. **DOK 3; MP.3**

Number of days	1	2	3	4	5
Earnings ($)	42	84	126	168	210

a. Complete the table.

b. Explain how you found the amounts that go in each cell of the table. Multiply days by $42.

c. Is this a proportional relationship? How do you know? Yes, there is a constant rate of change.

d. Write an equation to represent the relationship where x is the days worked and y is the dollars earned. $y = 42x$

2. **Draw Conclusions** Henry looks at a table that shows a proportional relationship. He notices that, in one column, the number of people is equal to the number of sandwiches eaten. What conclusion can he draw about the other cells in this table? Every cell must also show equal numbers for number of people and number of sandwiches eaten. **DOK 3; MP.7**

GETTING READY FOR GRADE 7

GR3.3 Proportional Relationships and Graphs

Engage

ESSENTIAL QUESTION

How can you tell if a graph represents a proportional relationship? A graph that is a line containing through the origin represents a proportional relationship.

Motivate the Lesson

Ask: What is another way, in addition to using a table of values, to tell whether a relationship is proportional? Begin the Explore Activity to find out.

Explore

EXPLORE ACTIVITY

Connect Vocabulary ELL

Make sure that students understand what *origin* means. Explain that the point named (0, 0) where the *x*- and *y*-axes meet is called the origin. Ask students to point to the origin on a graph.

Avoid Common Errors

Some students may see a straight-line graph and mistakenly assume that it has to represent a proportional relationship. Make sure that students understand that the origin must be a point on that line.

Explain

YOUR TURN

Avoid Common Errors

Exercise 2 Some students may incorrectly graph the point (1, 10) as (10, 1). Emphasize that the first step in using any graph is to read all the labels.

GETTING READY FOR GRADE 7

LESSON GR3.3 **Proportional Relationships and Graphs**

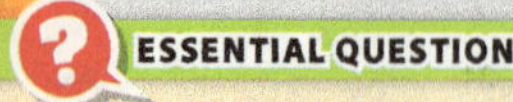

How can you tell if a graph represents a proportional relationship?

EXPLORE ACTIVITY

You can use a graph to decide if a relationship is a proportional relationship. If the graph has a line that starts at the origin, the relationship is proportional.

Students sell banners for $4 to raise money for their school. Is the relationship between the amount of money raised and the number of banners sold a proportional relationship?

A Complete the table to compare the amount raised to the number of banners sold.

Number Sold	1	2	3	5	8
Amount Raised ($)	4	8	12	20	32

B Based on the table, is this a proportional relationship? How do you know? Yes, the rate of change is constant at $4 per banner.

C Use the table to create a list of ordered pairs (number sold, money raised). (1, 4), (2, 8), (3, 12), (5, 20), (8, 32)

D Plot the ordered pairs.

E If no banners are sold, how much money will be raised? What is the ordered pair for this situation? If you draw a line to connect the points on the graph, does the line go through the origin? $0; (0, 0); yes

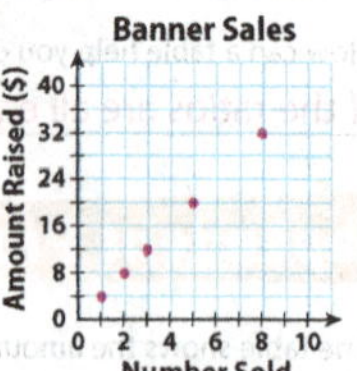

REFLECT

1. The table and the graph are different ways to show the relationship between the amount of money raised and the number of banners sold is proportional. How are they similar? How are they different? Both use the same set of points. The table, you must check whether the rate is constant. The graph, you have to see whether the points can be connected with a straight line that passes through the origin, (0, 0).

ADDITIONAL PRACTICE

Plot the ordered points on a graph and then tell whether or not the relationship is a proportional relationship.

1. (weeks, days): (2, 14), (4, 28), (5, 30), (7, 49) Yes

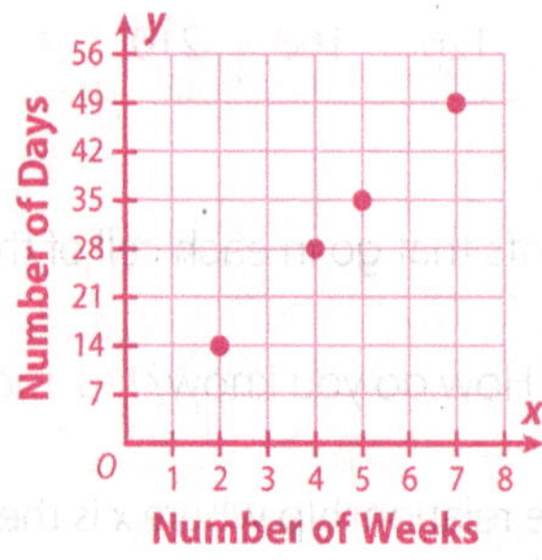

2. (months, height in inches): (6, 18), (9, 28), (12, 38), (15, 43) No

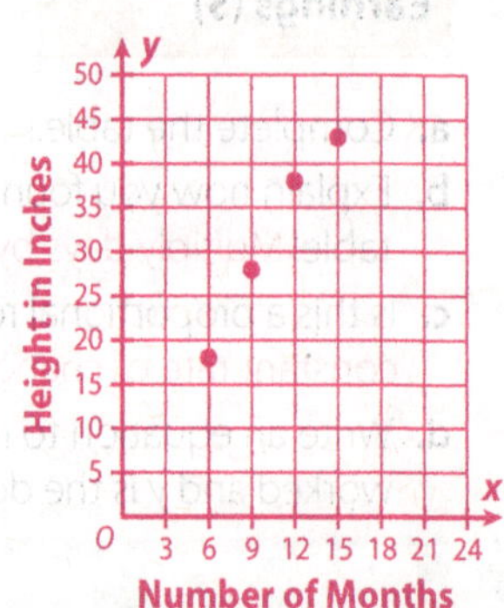

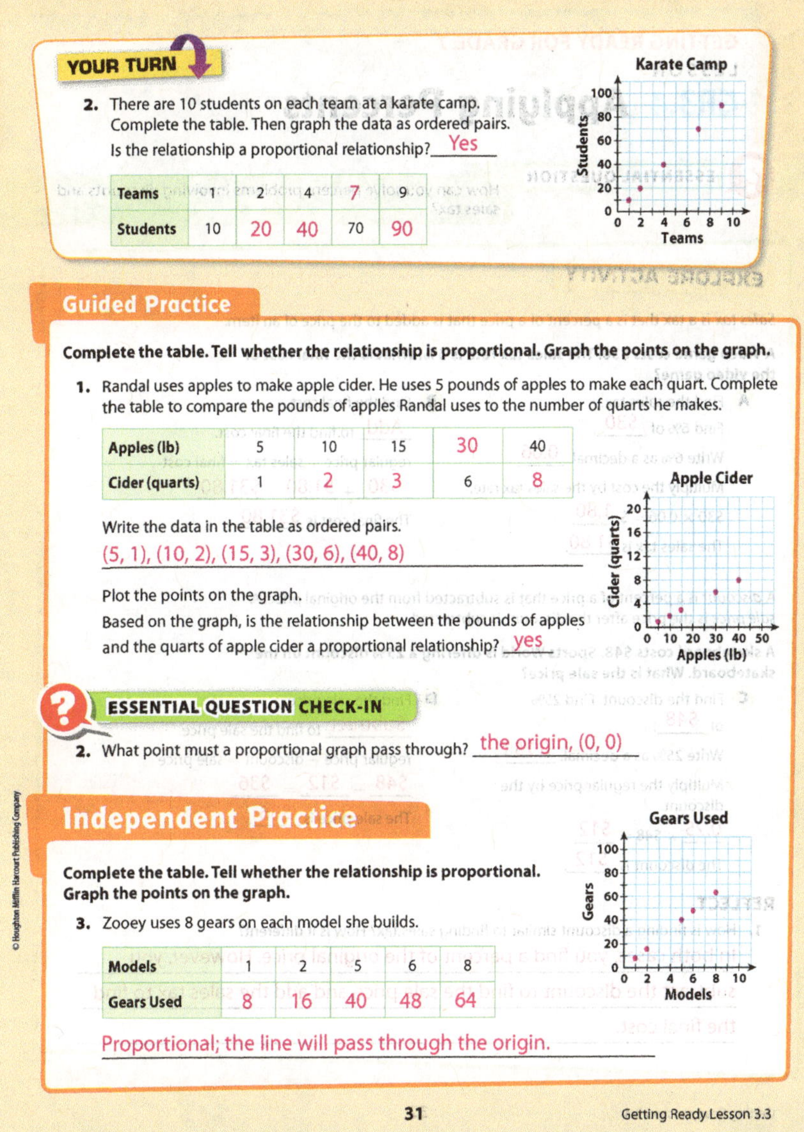

YOUR TURN

2. There are 10 students on each team at a karate camp. Complete the table. Then graph the data as ordered pairs. Is the relationship a proportional relationship? Yes

Teams	1	2	4	7	9
Students	10	20	40	70	90

Karate Camp
Students
Teams

Guided Practice

Complete the table. Tell whether the relationship is proportional. Graph the points on the graph.

1. Randal uses apples to make apple cider. He uses 5 pounds of apples to make each quart. Complete the table to compare the pounds of apples Randal uses to the number of quarts he makes.

Apples (lb)	5	10	15	30	40
Cider (quarts)	1	2	3	6	8

Write the data in the table as ordered pairs.
(5, 1), (10, 2), (15, 3), (30, 6), (40, 8)

Plot the points on the graph.
Based on the graph, is the relationship between the pounds of apples and the quarts of apple cider a proportional relationship? yes

Apple Cider
Cider (quarts)
Apples (lb)

ESSENTIAL QUESTION CHECK-IN

2. What point must a proportional graph pass through? the origin, (0, 0)

Independent Practice

Complete the table. Tell whether the relationship is proportional. Graph the points on the graph.

3. Zooey uses 8 gears on each model she builds.

Models	1	2	5	6	8
Gears Used	8	16	40	48	64

Proportional; the line will pass through the origin.

Gears Used
Gears
Models

31 Getting Ready Lesson 3.3

Elaborate

Talk About It **Summarize the Lesson**

Ask: How can you tell when a graph pictures a proportional relationship? To represent a proportional relationship, the graph must be a straight line that goes through the origin.

GUIDED PRACTICE

Questioning Strategies

- Why are the intervals used on the axes of the graph different for x and y? A greater interval is needed for the total apples because the values go from 5 to 40.
- What two characteristics do you look for in the graph in order to decide whether the relationship is proportional? The points form a line and the line goes through the origin, (0,0)

Evaluate

LESSON QUIZ

On each page of Kyle's album, he puts 4 photos.

1. Write 5 ordered points that represent this relationship. Sample answer: (0, 0), (1, 4), (2, 8), (3, 12), (4, 16)
2. Will your points be in a straight line on a graph? Yes.
3. Will the graph contain the origin? Yes.
4. Is this relationship a proportional relationship? Yes.

H.O.T. FOCUS ON HIGHER ORDER THINKING

1. **Represent Real-World Problems** Cynthia pays a $10 entry fee and $3 for each game she plays. Will the graph of this relationship (number of games she plays, total cost to her) be a straight line? Will the line contain the origin? Is this relationship a proportional relationship? Explain. Yes, it will be a straight line, but it will not contain the origin. Because her cost is $10 even if she plays 0 games, it is not a proportional relationship. **DOK 3; MP.7**

2. **Critical Thinking** Do the units marked on the *x*-axis and the *y*-axis have to be the same in order for the graph to represent a proportional relationship? Explain. No, the units do not have to be the same as long as there is a constant ratio, it forms a line, and goes through the origin. **DOK 3; MP.7**

GETTING READY FOR GRADE 7

GR3.4 Applying Percents

Engage

ESSENTIAL QUESTION

How can you solve percent problems involving discounts and sales tax? To find the amount of discount or tax, first find the percent of the base number. Then add or subtract that percent amount to find the total cost with tax or the sale price after the discount.

Motivate the Lesson

Ask: Have you ever wondered how to find out the cost of something that has a discount? Begin the Explore Activity to find out.

Explore

EXPLORE ACTIVITY Connect Vocabulary ELL

The meaning and use of the word *percent* may not be clear to some students. Remind students that *percent* means *per hundred*, so 6% means 6 per 100. As a tax rate, this means 6 cents for every hundred cents, or dollar.

Explain

YOUR TURN Avoid Common Errors

Exercise 3 Some students may think that they only have to pay 15% of $50. Explain that the discount, or amount subtracted, is 15% of $50, and what they have to pay is the amount remaining after the discount is subtracted from the regular, or original, price.

GETTING READY FOR GRADE 7

LESSON

GR3.4 Applying Percents

ESSENTIAL QUESTION

How can you solve percent problems involving discounts and sales tax?

EXPLORE ACTIVITY

Sales tax is a tax that is a percent of a price that is added to the price of an item.

A video game costs $30. The sales tax rate is 6%. What is the final cost of the video game?

A Find the sales tax.

Find 6% of $30.

Write 6% as a decimal. 0.06

Multiply the cost by the sales tax rate.

$30 × 0.06 = $1.80.

The sales tax is $1.80.

B Find the final cost.

Add to find the final cost.

regular price + sales tax = final cost

$30 + $1.80 = $31.80

The final cost is $31.80.

A *discount* is a percent of a price that is subtracted from the original price. A *sale price* is the price after the discount is subtracted.

A skateboard costs $48. Sports World is offering a 25% discount on the skateboard. What is the sale price?

C Find the discount. Find 25% of $48.

Write 25% as a decimal. 0.25

Multiply the regular price by the discount.

0.25 × $48 = $12

The discount is $12.

D Find the sale price.

Subtract to find the sale price.

regular price − discount = sale price

$48 − $12 = $36

The sale price is $36.

REFLECT

1. How is finding a discount similar to finding sales tax? How is it different?

In both cases, you find a percent of the original price. However, you subtract the discount to find the sale price and add the sales tax to find the final cost.

ADDITIONAL PRACTICE

1. Write 8% as a decimal. 0.08
2. Write 30% as a decimal. 0.30 or 0.3
3. A coat cost $30 and the sales tax rate is 6%. What is the amount of the tax? $1.80
4. The original price of a shirt is $20 and the discount is 15%. What is the amount of the discount? $3.00
5. The original price of a book is $10 and the discount is 20%. What is the amount of the discount? $2.00
6. A sandwich cost $2.50 and the sales tax rate is 6%. What is the amount of the tax? $0.15
7. A water bottle cost $12 and the sales tax rate is 7%. What is the final cost? $12.84
8. The original price of a book bag is $24 and the discount is 15%. What is the sales price? $20.40
9. A meal cost $7.80 and the sales tax rate is 5%. What is the final cost? $8.19
10. The original price of a poster is $14 and the discount is 10%. What is the sale price? $12.60

YOUR TURN

2. A graphic novel costs $24. The sales tax is 5%. What is the final cost of the graphic novel? $25.20

3. A jacket regularly costs $50. It is discounted 15%. What is the sale price of the jacket? $42.50

Guided Practice

1. A sports shirt costs $32 plus tax. The sales tax is 8%. What is the sales tax?
Find 8% of 32.
8% = 0.08 *Change 8% to a decimal.*
0.08 × $32 = $2.56 *Multiply to get sales tax.*

2. Find the final cost of the sports shirt.
Regular price + Sales tax = Final Cost
$32 + $2.56 = $34.56

ESSENTIAL QUESTION CHECK-IN

3. How do you find a sale price?
Change the discount percent to a decimal and multiply by the regular price. Then subtract the discount from the regular price.

Independent Practice

Find the sales tax and the final cost.

4. Soccer ball: $18
Sales tax rate: 3%
Sales tax: $0.54
Final cost: $18.54

5. Remote control car: $52
Sales tax rate: 8%
Sales tax: $4.16
Final cost: $56.16

6. Sneakers: $35
Sales tax rate: 7%
Sales tax: $2.45
Final cost: $37.45

Find the discount and the sale price.

7. Tennis racket: $18
Discount percent: 20%
Discount amount: $3.60
Sale price: $14.40

8. Jeans: $26
Discount percent: 10%
Discount amount: $2.60
Sale price: $23.40

9. Lamp: $53
Discount percent: 25%
Discount amount: $13.25
Sale price: $39.75

10. Which costs less, a shirt that regularly sells for $20 that is discounted 10% or a shirt that regularly sells for $24 that is discounted 20%? How do you know?
The discounted $20 shirt; $18 is less than $19.20.

33 Getting Ready Lesson 3.4

Elaborate

Connect Vocabulary ELL

Some students may confuse *discount* with *sale price*. Explain that a discount is often written as a percent off, such *20% off*, meaning that 20% of the original price will be taken off, or subtracted, to find the (lower) sale price.

Talk About It **Summarize the Lesson**

Ask: How is the process for finding the sale price after a discount different from the process for finding the total cost, including tax? The amount of a discount is subtracted and the amount of tax is added.

GUIDED PRACTICE Avoid Common Errors

Exercises 1 Some students may think incorrectly that 8% can be written as 0.8 because, for example, 25% is correctly written as 0.25. Explain that you do *not* simply erase the percent sign and put a decimal point in front. Emphasize the meaning of percent means "per hundred".

Evaluate

LESSON QUIZ

Find the sales tax and the final cost.

1. A book with a price of $15 and a sales tax of 4%. $0.60; $15.60

2. A lamp with a price of $30 and a sales tax of 7%. $2.10; $32.10

Find the discount and the sale price.

3. A game with a price of $18 and a discount of 10%. $1.80; $16.20

4. A toy with a price of $9 and a discount of 15%. $1.35; $7.65

H.O.T. FOCUS ON HIGHER ORDER THINKING

1. **Represent Real-World Problems** How could a discount of 25% be expressed in an advertisement as a fraction? Sample answer: $\frac{1}{4}$ off. **DOK 2; MP.3**

2. **Analyze Relationships** The cost of snack shared equally by 4 people is $18.00. They want to leave a tip of 15%. How much should each person pay? Explain. 15% of $18 is $2.70. $18 + $2.70 = $20.70. The total cost of $20.70 shared equally by 4 people is $5.18 (rounded up to the nearest penny). **DOK 3; MP.4**

3. **Communicate Mathematical Ideas** Can the sale price of an item ever be less than the amount of the discount? Explain. Yes, for example, if the original price is $100 and the discount is 75%, then the discount amount is $75 and the sale price is $100 − $75 = $25. $25 < $75. **DOK 3; MP.3**

4. **Analyze Relationships** The final cost for a book is $10.50. The price of the book is $10. What is the tax rate? Explain. The tax amount is $0.50. To find the rate, divide $0.50 by $10, which gives a rate of 0.05 or 5%. **DOK 3; MP.4**

GETTING READY FOR GRADE 7

GR3.5 Finding Percent of Change

Engage

ESSENTIAL QUESTION

How can you determine the percent of change and determine if it is an increase or a decrease? Divide the amount of the change by the original number. If the new amount is greater than the original amount, then it is an increase. If the new amount is less than the original amount, then it is a decrease.

Motivate the Lesson

Ask: What does it mean to have an 80% increase in something? Begin the Explore Activity to find out.

Explore

EXPLORE ACTIVITY

Questioning Strategies **Mathematical Processes and Practices**

- How do you find the amount of change? Subtract the lesser value from the greater value.
- How do you know if it is a percent of increase or a percent of decrease? If the new amount is greater than the original amount, then it is an increase. If the new amount is less than the original amount, then it is a decrease.

Explain

YOUR TURN

Avoid Common Errors

Exercise 2 Remind students that when changing a fraction to a decimal, the top number is divided by the bottom number. For example $\frac{1}{3}$ means $1 \div 3$ or $3\overline{)1}$.

GETTING READY FOR GRADE 7

LESSON GR3.5 **Finding Percent of Change**

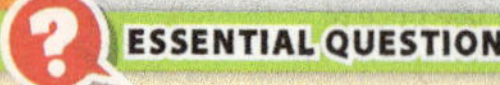

ESSENTIAL QUESTION

How can you determine the percent of change and determine if it is an increase or a decrease?

EXPLORE ACTIVITY

A percent can describe an increase or a decrease in an amount that has changed. The process for finding both is the same.

$$\text{Percent Change} = \frac{\text{Amount of Change}}{\text{Original Amount}}$$

If the change is greater than the original amount, it is a percent increase. If the change is less than the original amount, it is a percent decrease.

The price of a video game increases from $20 to $25. What is the percent increase?

A Find the amount of change.

Amount of Change = Greater Value − Lesser Value

= 25 − 20 Substitute values.

= 5 Subtract.

B Find the percent increase. Round to the nearest percent.

$\text{Percent Change} = \frac{\text{Amount of Change}}{\text{Original Amount}} = \frac{5}{20}$ Substitute values.

= 0.25 Divide.

= 25% Write as a percent and round.

Tanner decreased the length of his garden from 35 feet to 30 feet. What is the percent decrease?

C Find the amount of change.

Amount of Change = Greater Value − Lesser Value

= 35 − 30 Substitute values.

= 5 Subtract.

D Find the percent decrease. Round to the nearest percent.

$\text{Percent Change} = \frac{\text{Amount of Change}}{\text{Original Amount}} = \frac{5}{35}$ Substitute values.

= 14% Write as a percent and round.

REFLECT

1. What is 25% of $20? How can you use this to check that the percent increase from $20 to $25 is 25%?
25% of $20 is $5, which is the amount of increase from $20 to $25.

ADDITIONAL PRACTICE

Find the percent of change to the nearest percent. Tell whether it is an increase or decrease.

1. Original amount: 20
New amount: 30 50%; increase
2. Original amount: 40
New amount: 20 50%; decrease
3. Original amount: 100
New amount: 70 30%; decrease
4. Original amount: 80
New amount: 92 15%; increase
5. Original amount: 85
New amount: 119 40%; increase
6. Original amount: 45
New amount: 30 33%; decrease
7. Original amount: 36
New amount: 52 44%; increase
8. Original amount: 98
New amount: 76 22%; decrease

YOUR TURN

2. Annie's puppy weighs 18 pounds at 6 months. At one year, her dog weighs 24 pounds. What is the percent increase? 33%

3. The price of a pair of pants decreases from \$45 to \$36. What is the percent decrease? 20%

Guided Practice

1. The price of a pair of roller skates changes from \$60 to \$70.

Is the change an increase or decrease? increase

70 − 60 = 10 *Find the amount of change.*

$\text{Percent Change} = \frac{\text{Amount of Change}}{\text{Original Amount}} = \frac{10}{60}$ *Substitute values.*

= 17% *Round and write as a percent.*

ESSENTIAL QUESTION CHECK-IN

2. How do you find a percent change?

Sample answer: Find the difference between the original amount and the new amount. Then write the ratio of the amount of change to the original amount. Divide to write the ratio as a decimal and then write the percent.

Independent Practice

Find the percent of change. Tell whether it is an increase or a decrease.

3. Original amount: 50
New amount: 80
60%; increase

4. Original amount: 40
New amount: 35
13%; decrease

5. Original amount: 28
New amount: 18
36%; decrease

6. The price of a DVD was originally \$30. It is on sale for \$18. What is the percent change? Is it an increase or decrease? 40%; decrease

7. The cost of a painting doubles from \$40 to \$80. Predict the percent increase without calculating. Then find the actual percent increase. Does your prediction match the actual percent increase? Explain.

The percent increase is 100%. My prediction matches the percent increase because the amount of change is equal to the original amount.

Elaborate

Talk About It Summarize the Lesson

Ask: How do you find a percent change and decide if it is an increase or decrease? Find the difference between the original amount and the changed amount. The percent change is the ratio of the amount of change to the original amount, written as a percent. If the changed amount is greater than the original, it is an increase. If it is less than the original amount, it is a decrease.

GUIDED PRACTICE

Avoid Common Errors

Exercise 1 Point out that students need only find the percent change to the nearest percent. This means students must divide to the hundredths place if the division does not terminate. Then they can round to the nearest percent. If students use a calculator to divide, remind them to look only up to the hundredths place to round when necessary.

Focus on Math Connections **Mathematical Processes and Practices**

Discuss how to use number sense to check that the percent change makes sense. Have students find 10% of \$60, which is \$6. So, 20% of \$60 is \$12. Since 17% is less than 20%, \$10 is a reasonable estimate of 17% and is consistent with the increase from \$60 to \$70.

Evaluate

LESSON QUIZ

Find each percent of change to the nearest percent. Is it an increase or decrease?

1. Original amount: 25
New amount: 15
40%; decrease

2. Original amount: 20
New amount: 32
60%; increase

3. Original amount: 58
New amount: 68
17%; increase

4. Original amount: 12
New amount: 8
33%; decrease

FOCUS ON HIGHER ORDER THINKING

1. **Communicate Mathematical Ideas** Suppose an amount increases by 10%, then decreases by 10%. Is the final amount the original amount? Explain your thinking. No, the final amount is less than the original amount. For example, 10% of 50 is 5, so 55 is a 10% increase from 50. 10% of 55 is 5.5, so 49.5 is a 10% decrease from 55. **DOK 3; MP.2**

2. **Critical Thinking** Explain why a change in price from \$40 to \$20 is a 50% decrease, but a change in price from \$20 to \$40 is a 100% increase. In both cases the amount of change is \$20 but the original price is different. For the percent decrease, $\frac{20}{40} = 50\%$ but for the percent increase, $\frac{20}{20} = 100\%$. **DOK 3; MP.2**

GETTING READY FOR GRADE 7

GR3.6 Finding Simple Interest

Engage

ESSENTIAL QUESTION

How can you find simple interest for a year? Possible answer: To find simple interest for a year, multiply the interest rate by the initial amount.

Motivate the Lesson

Ask: One of the reasons people put money in a savings account is to earn interest on the money they are saving. The money earned is called interest. Begin the Explore Activity to find out.

Explore

EXPLORE ACTIVITY Focus on Reasoning

Emphasize that regardless of how many years the interest is being calculated, the interest rate is multiplied by the initial deposit. The only time that would change is if the deposit changes.

Explain

YOUR TURN Questioning Strategies

- What information do you need to compute the simple interest on the original amount called the principle? the interest rate and the number of years
- Why is it necessary to write the interest rate as a decimal? the percent has to be changed to a decimal to multiply

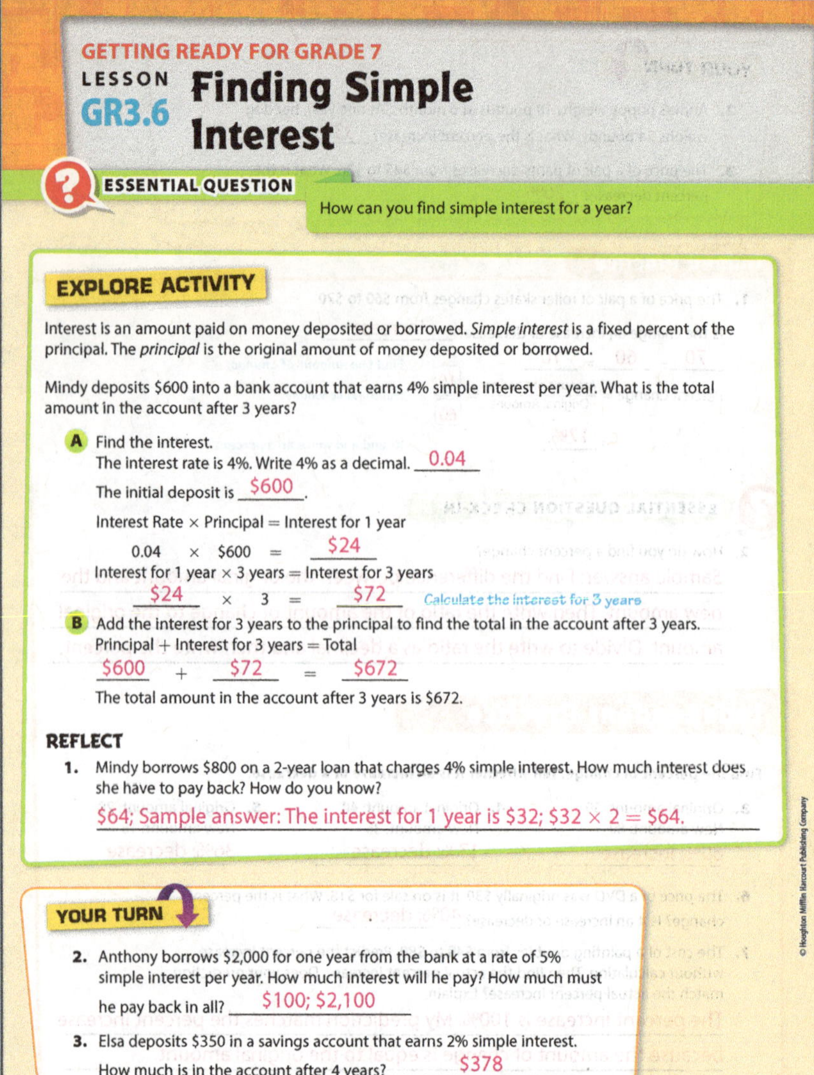

GETTING READY FOR GRADE 7

LESSON GR3.6 Finding Simple Interest

ESSENTIAL QUESTION

How can you find simple interest for a year?

EXPLORE ACTIVITY

Interest is an amount paid on money deposited or borrowed. *Simple interest* is a fixed percent of the principal. The *principal* is the original amount of money deposited or borrowed.

Mindy deposits $600 into a bank account that earns 4% simple interest per year. What is the total amount in the account after 3 years?

A Find the interest.

The interest rate is 4%. Write 4% as a decimal. 0.04

The initial deposit is $600.

Interest Rate × Principal = Interest for 1 year

0.04 × $600 = $24

Interest for 1 year × 3 years = Interest for 3 years

$24 × 3 = $72 Calculate the interest for 3 years

B Add the interest for 3 years to the principal to find the total in the account after 3 years.

Principal + Interest for 3 years = Total

$600 + $72 = $672

The total amount in the account after 3 years is $672.

REFLECT

1. Mindy borrows $800 on a 2-year loan that charges 4% simple interest. How much interest does she have to pay back? How do you know?
$64; Sample answer: The interest for 1 year is $32; $32 × 2 = $64.

YOUR TURN

2. Anthony borrows $2,000 for one year from the bank at a rate of 5% simple interest per year. How much interest will he pay? How much must he pay back in all? $100; $2,100

3. Elsa deposits $350 in a savings account that earns 2% simple interest. How much is in the account after 4 years? $378

© Houghton Mifflin Harcourt Publishing Company

Getting Ready Lesson 3.6 36

ADDITIONAL PRACTICE

1. Cameron borrows $400 from the bank at a rate of 8% simple interest for 1 year. How much interest will he be charged? $32

2. Lucia deposits $50 in a savings account that earns 3% simple interest for 10 years. How much interest will the account earn? $15

3. Felipe has $300 in an account that earns 5% simple interest. How much interest will he have in the account after 2 years? $330

4. Uta borrows $1,000 on a 2-year loan at a rate of 8% simple interest. How much must she pay back in all? $1,160

5. Lizzie deposits $200 in a savings account that earns 4% simple interest. How much is in the account after 3 years? $224

6. Jonny borrows $1,500 from the bank at a rate of 7% simple interest for 5 years. What is the total cost of the loan? $2,025

7. Angela borrows $900 at a rate of 10% simple interest for a 4-year loan. How much will Angela pay back in all? $1,260

8. Barry deposits $250 in an account that earns 3% simple interest for 5 years. What is the total amount in the account after 5 years? $287.50

Guided Practice

1. Devon borrowed $3,500 from the bank at a rate of 7% simple interest per year. How much interest does he pay in 5 years? What is the total amount he has to pay back?

STEP 1 Find the amount of interest for one year.
Then calculate the amount of interest for 5 years.
Interest Rate × Principal = Interest for 1 year
0.07 × $3,500 = $245
Interest for 1 year × 5 years = Interest for 5 years
$245 × 5 = $1,225

STEP 2 Add the interest for 5 years to the principal to find the total cost Devon has to pay back.
Principal + Interest for 5 years = Total
$3,500 + $1,225 = $4,725

ESSENTIAL QUESTION CHECK-IN

2. How do you find the simple interest on a 5-year loan?
Sample answer: Multiply the interest rate by the principal, which is the original amount of the deposit or loan. Then multiply the interest by 5, the length of the loan.

Independent Practice

3. Julio deposits $700 in a bank account that earns 3% simple interest. How much interest does the account earn in 6 years? How much is in the account after 6 years?
$126; $826

4. Nathan borrows $800 at a rate of 10% simple interest for a 5-year loan. What will be the total amount he will have to pay back?
$1,200

5. Jason deposits $500 in an account that earns 3% simple interest for 2 years. At the end of the two years, he has to close the account. He then deposits the total into a different account that earns 2% interest for 2 years. How much does he have in all at the end of the 4 years? Explain your thinking.
The interest on the first account is $30, so at the end of 2 years, he has $530. The interest on $530 in the second account is $21.20. At the end of 4 years, he has $551.20.

Elaborate

Talk About It Summarize the Lesson

Ask: Given the original amount of a deposit or a loan, how do you find the simple interest due after one year? Multiply the original amount by the interest rate, expressed as a decimal.

GUIDED PRACTICE

Avoid Common Errors

Exercise 1 Students may have trouble converting percents less than 10%. Emphasize that percent means per hundred.

Focus on Reasoning

Emphasize that regardless of how many years the interest is being calculated, the interest rate is multiplied by the original amount borrowed (or deposited), provided that initial amount does not change.

Evaluate

LESSON QUIZ

1. Iris deposits $800 in an account that earns 4% simple interest. How much interest does the account earn in 5 years? $160
2. Joey borrows $600 at a rate of 12% simple interest. How much interest will he pay back in 3 years? $216
3. Kareem deposits $1,200 in an account that earns 3% simple interest. What is the total amount in the account after 4 years? $1,344
4. Tanya borrows $400 at a rate of 9% simple interest for a 2-year loan. What will be the total cost of the loan? $472

H.O.T. FOCUS ON HIGHER ORDER THINKING

1. **Represent Real-World Problems** Rosa deposits $1,000 in an account that pays 3% annual interest. The next year she re-deposits the amount with the interest earned back in the account. How much is in her account at the end of 2 years? Explain. First year end amount: $1,030; Second year end amount: $1,060.90 **DOK 3; MP.3**

2. **Analyze Relationships** Josh wants to borrow $900. He can take out a 4-year loan with an interest rate of 6% or he can take out a 5-year loan with an interest rate of 5%. Which is the better choice? Explain your thinking. Possible answer: The 4-year loan has $216 interest to pay while the 5-year loan has $225 interest to pay. $216 < $225, the 4-year loan is better. **DOK 2; MP.3**

3. **Analyze Relationships** Natalie and Kyle compared the amount of interest they earned on their saving accounts. Each initially deposited $500. Natalie earned $25 and Kyle earned $22.50. Whose account paid the higher interest rate? How do you know? Natalie's account because the higher interest rate yields a greater amount of interest and $25 > $22.50. **DOK 3; MP.3**

4. **Represent Real-World Problems** Diego's savings account earned $36 simple interest in 2 years. The account paid 6% simple interest. What was his initial deposit? $300; $36 ÷ 0.06 = $600; $600 ÷ 2 = $300 **DOK 2; MP.3**

GETTING READY FOR GRADE 7

GR4.1 Algebraic Expressions

Engage

ESSENTIAL QUESTION

How can you model factoring expressions? I can arrange algebra tiles to form a rectangle and multiply the length by the width.

Motivate the Lesson

Ask: An algebraic expression contains a variable. Sometimes an algebraic expression can be written differently by factoring. What does it mean to factor an algebraic expression? Begin the Explore Activity to find out.

Explore

EXPLORE ACTIVITY Questioning Strategies

- What are the dimensions of each tile? The *x*-tile is *x* units long and 1 unit wide. The 1-tiles are 1 unit long and 1 unit wide.
- What do the dimensions of the rectangle represent? the factors

Explain

YOUR TURN

Focus on Modeling **Mathematical Processes and Practices**

Have students use algebra tiles to model each exercise. Point out that as the coefficients and constants get larger, modeling becomes more cumbersome. Remind students to write the numerical factor to the left of the algebraic factor and that the parentheses indicate multiplication.

Avoid Common Errors

Exercise 2 Some students may factor the expression as $4(x + 1)$ while others may write $2(2x + 2)$. Explain that the correct answer is found by placing the greatest common factor outside the parentheses.

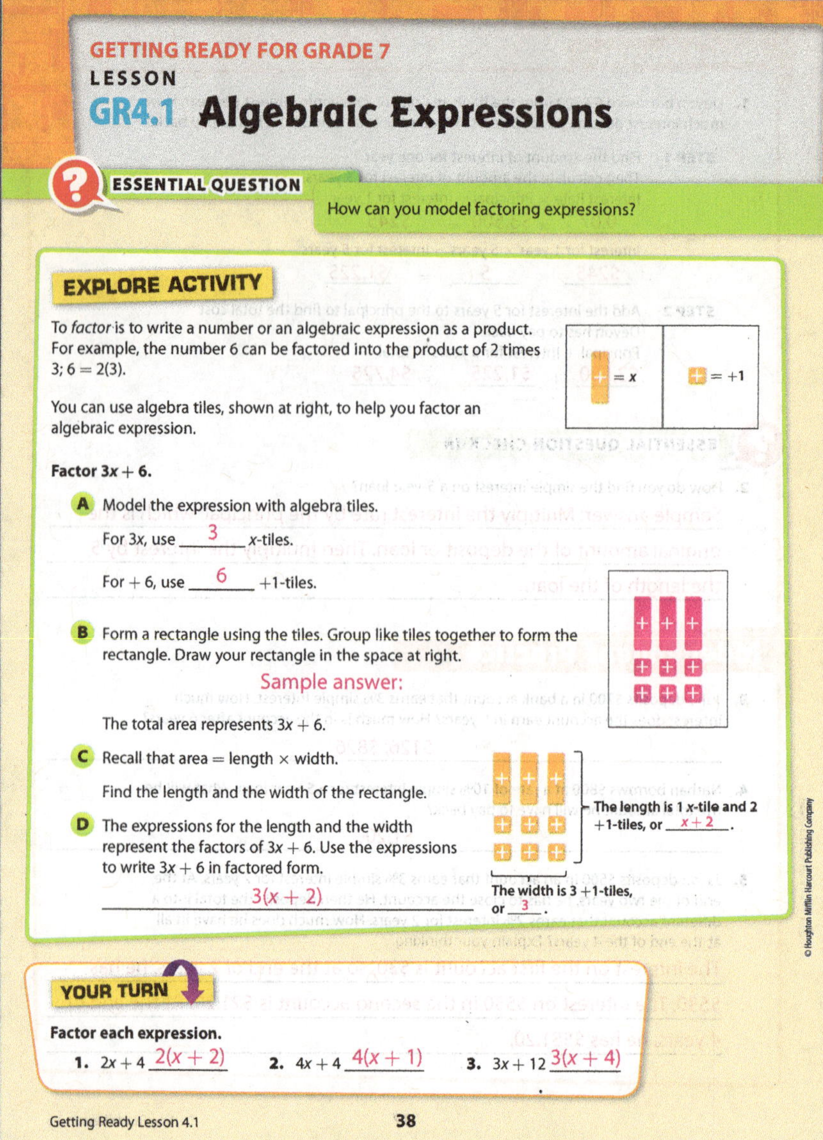
GETTING READY FOR GRADE 7

LESSON

GR4.1 Algebraic Expressions

ESSENTIAL QUESTION

How can you model factoring expressions?

EXPLORE ACTIVITY

To *factor* is to write a number or an algebraic expression as a product. For example, the number 6 can be factored into the product of 2 times 3; $6 = 2(3)$.

You can use algebra tiles, shown at right, to help you factor an algebraic expression.

Factor $3x + 6$.

A Model the expression with algebra tiles.

For $3x$, use 3 *x*-tiles.

For $+ 6$, use 6 +1-tiles.

B Form a rectangle using the tiles. Group like tiles together to form the rectangle. Draw your rectangle in the space at right.

Sample answer:

The total area represents $3x + 6$.

C Recall that area = length × width.

Find the length and the width of the rectangle.

D The expressions for the length and the width represent the factors of $3x + 6$. Use the expressions to write $3x + 6$ in factored form.

$3(x + 2)$

YOUR TURN

Factor each expression.

1. $2x + 4$ $2(x + 2)$
2. $4x + 4$ $4(x + 1)$
3. $3x + 12$ $3(x + 4)$

Getting Ready Lesson 4.1 38

ADDITIONAL PRACTICE

Factor each expression.

1. $2x + 8$ $2(x + 4)$
2. $3x + 3$ $3(x + 1)$
3. $4x + 16$ $4(x + 4)$
4. $6x + 6$ $6(x + 1)$
5. $2x + 6$ $2(x + 3)$
6. $7x + 14$ $7(x + 2)$
7. $4x + 20$ $4(x + 5)$
8. $3x + 18$ $3(x + 6)$
9. $5x + 15$ $5(x + 3)$
10. $8x + 16$ $8(x + 2)$

Guided Practice

1. Factor $2x + 6$.

How many tiles do you need?

2 x-tiles and 6 +1-tiles

Arrange the tiles into a rectangle. Draw your rectangle in the space at right. Sample answer:

What is the length of the rectangle? 1 x-tile and 3 +1-tiles, or $x + 3$

What is the width of the rectangle? 2 +1-tiles, or 2

Write $2x + 6$ in factored form. $2(x + 3)$

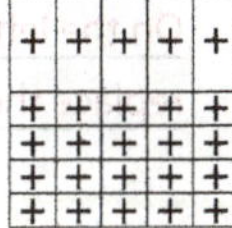

ESSENTIAL QUESTION CHECK-IN

2. How can algebra tiles help you factor an algebraic expression?

Sample answer: Model the expression using the tiles. Then form the tiles into a rectangle. The length and width of the rectangle represent the factors of the expression.

Independent Practice

Factor each expression.

3. $2x + 2$ $2(x + 1)$
4. $3x + 9$ $3(x + 3)$
5. $4x + 8$ $4(x + 2)$
6. $5x + 10$ $5(x + 2)$
7. $4x + 12$ $4(x + 3)$
8. $3x + 15$ $3(x + 5)$

9. The area of a square can be represented by the expression $2x + 10$. What are two factors that could represent its length and width?

Sample answer: 2 and $x + 5$

10. Candace drew the diagram shown at the right to factor an expression. If the shapes represent algebra tiles, what expression did she factor? What are its factors? Explain.

$5x + 20$; $5(x + 4)$; In algebra tiles, rectangles represent x and squares represent +1. So the length is $x + 4$ and the width is 5.

Elaborate

Talk About It

Summarize the Lesson

Ask: How does modeling an expression with algebra tiles help you factor the expression? By making a rectangle with the algebra tiles, the length and width of the rectangle are the factors of the expression.

GUIDED PRACTICE

Engage with the Whiteboard

Ask student volunteers to draw tiles to represent their rectangles. Have them explain how they identified the length and width from their models.

Avoid Common Errors

Exercise 1 Remind students to check that they have factored correctly by using the distributive property to find the product of the factors. The product must be equal to the original expression.

Evaluate

LESSON QUIZ

Factor each expression.

1. $3x + 12$ $3(x + 4)$
2. $2x + 10$ $2(x + 5)$
3. $4x + 12$ $4(x + 3)$
4. $5x + 5$ $5(x + 1)$
5. $6x + 12$ $6(x + 2)$

H.O.T. FOCUS ON HIGHER ORDER THINKING

1. **Analyze Relationships** An algebra tile that represents −1 is similar to the algebra tile that represents +1, except that is has the minus sign "−" on the tile rather than the plus sign. How would you use algebra tiles to represent and factor $2x - 2$? Use two x-tiles and two −1-tiles. Make a rectangle. The factors are 2 and $x - 1$. **DOK 3; MP.4**

2. **Analyze Relationships** Is the expression $4(2x + 2)$ fully factored? How do you know? What is the fully factored expression? No, because $2x + 2$ can be factored again; $8(x + 1)$ **DOK 3; MP.7**

3. **Critical Thinking** Wanda models a rectangle with a length of $2x + 6$ and a width of 3. What is the area of the rectangle? What are the factors of the expression that represents the area? Explain. Area is $(2x + 6)(3) = 6x + 18$ and $6x + 18 = 6(x + 3)$. **DOK 3; MP.4**

4. **Multiple Representations** Xavier uses four x-tiles and six +1-tiles to make a rectangle. What algebraic expression does the rectangle represent? What are the factors of the expression? $4x + 6$; $2(2x + 3)$ **DOK 2; MP.4**

GETTING READY FOR GRADE 7

GR4.2 Modeling Two-Step Equations

Engage

ESSENTIAL QUESTION

How can you model two-step equations? I can use algebra tiles to model two-step equations.

Motivate the Lesson

Ask: You have used algebra tiles to model algebraic expressions. How do you think the algebra tiles might be used to model equations? Begin the Explore Activity to find out.

Explore

EXPLORE ACTIVITY

Focus on Communication **Mathematical Processes and Practices**

Since positive signs and negative signs are found on more than one algebra tile, remind students to use descriptive terms when talking about the tiles. Using the phrases "positive variable tile" and "−1" tile," will make talking about their models easier.

Explain

YOUR TURN Questioning Strategies

- What tiles do you use to model the left side of the equation? Where do you put the models? Use four positive variable tiles and two −1-tiles. These tiles go in the left box on the mat.
- What part of the mat represents the equal sign? the center line
- What tiles do you use to model the right side of the equation? Where do you put the models? Use six +1-tiles. These tiles go in the right box on the mat.

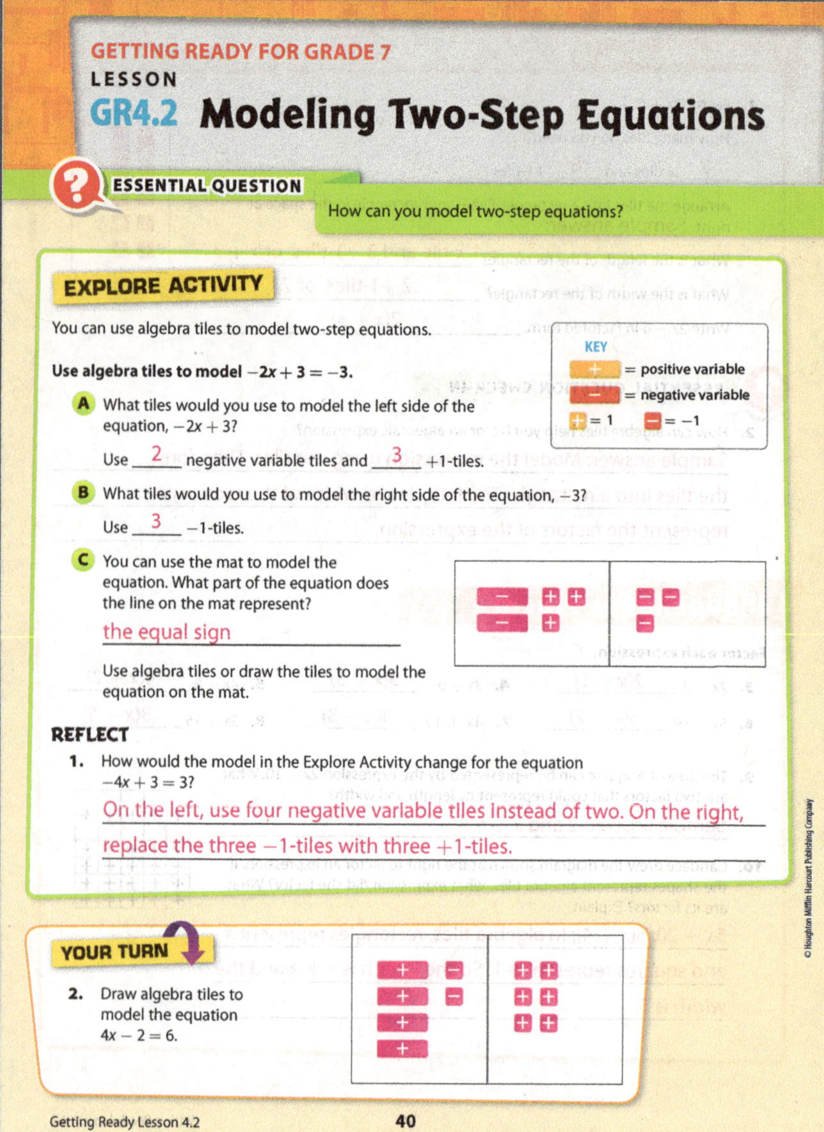

ADDITIONAL PRACTICE

Draw algebra tiles to model the given two-step equations.

1. $3x + 1 = -2$

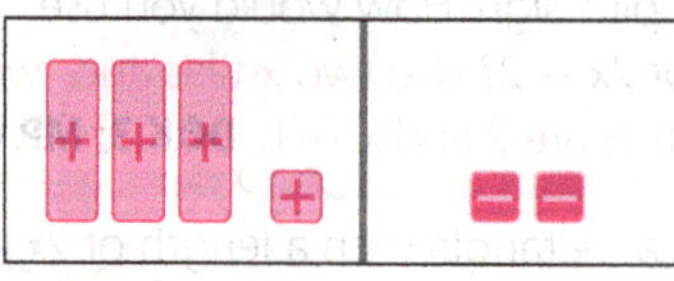

2. $4x + 5 = -1$

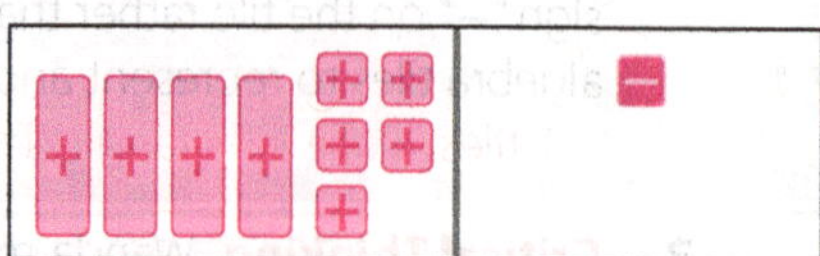

3. $2x + 4 = 6$

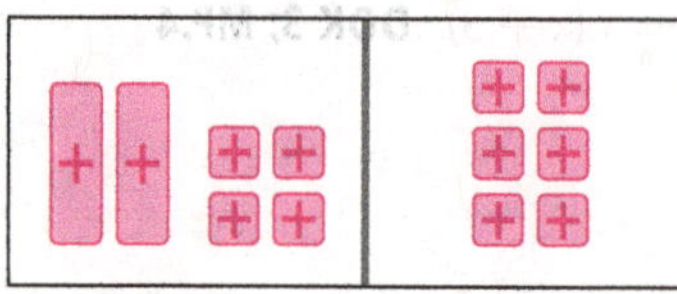

4. $-3x + 2 = -4$

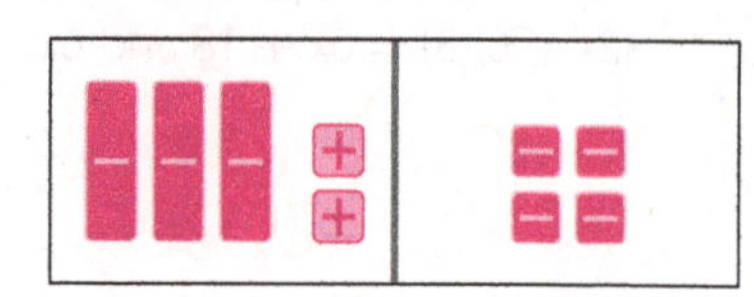

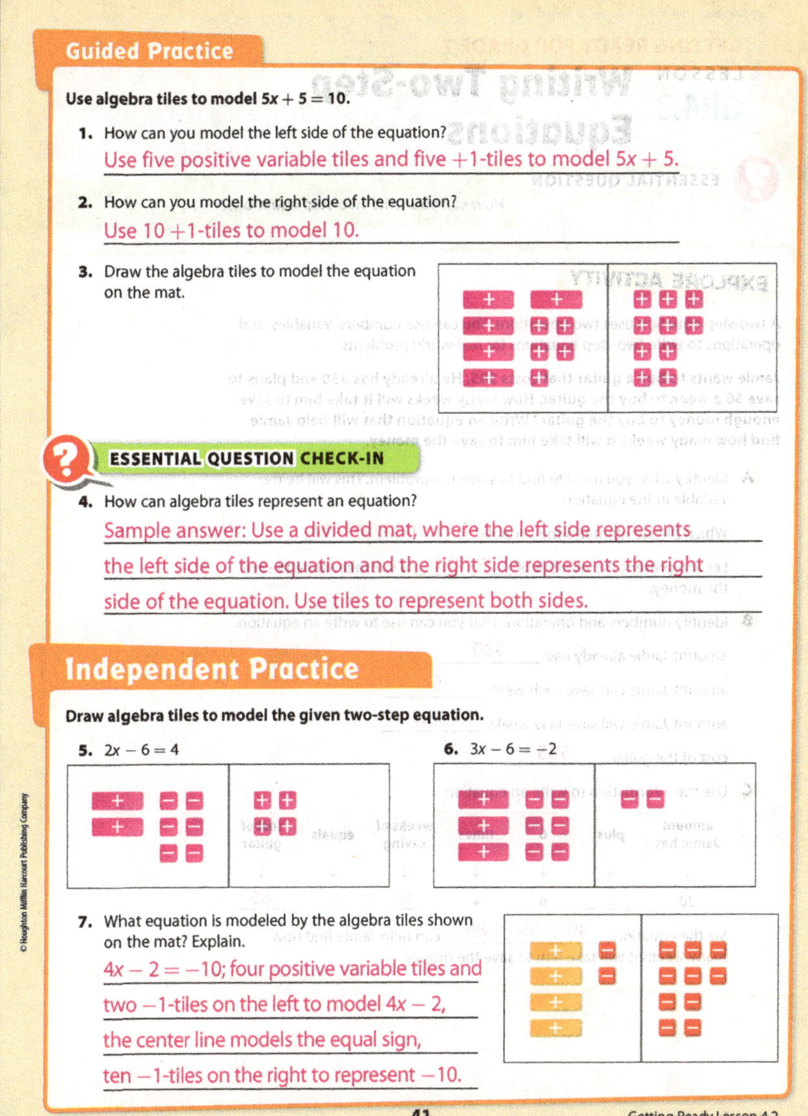

Elaborate

Talk About It

Summarize the Lesson

Ask: Why is it helpful to model an expression with algebra tiles? Modeling the expression is having a picture of the problem and helping visualize the steps needed to solve.

GUIDED PRACTICE

Avoid Common Errors

Exercise 3 Remind students to model each side separately rather than selecting all the tiles needed at once so they do not confuse the tiles. For example, model the left hand side completely before modeling the right hand side. This will also serve to remind them which part of the mat to use.

Evaluate

LESSON QUIZ

Draw algebra tiles to model the given two-step equations.

1. $-2x + 6 = 2$

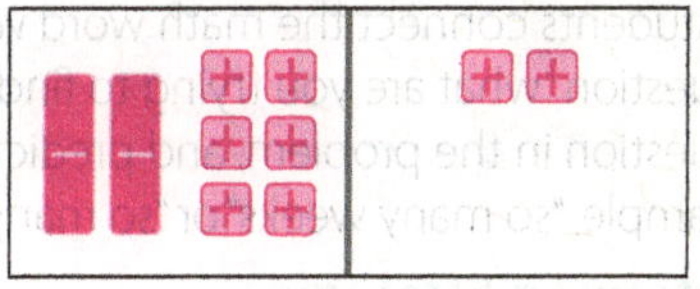

2. $4x - 3 = 5$

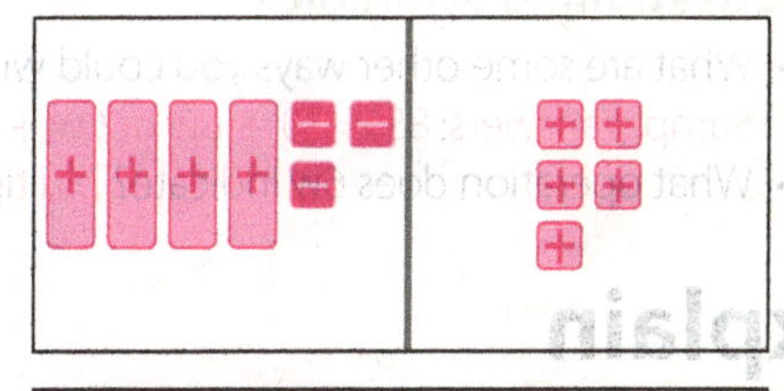

3. $-3x - 4 = 2$

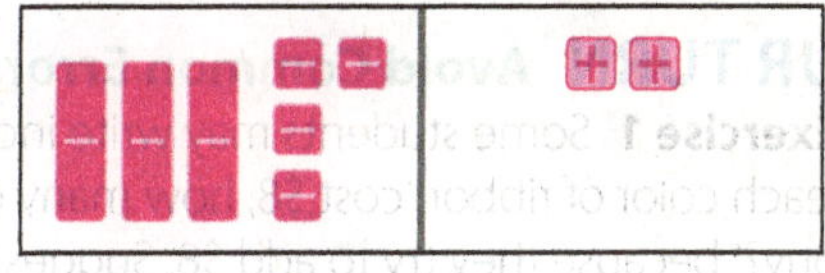

H.O.T. FOCUS ON HIGHER ORDER THINKING

1. **Analyze Relationships** How are the models for the equations $4x + 2 = -2$ and $-4x - 2 = 2$ similar? What do you think this means about the solutions of the equations? Sample answer: They use the same number of opposite tiles. This means they should have the same solution. **DOK 3; MP.4**

2. **Analyze Relationships** Consider the equation $3x + 2 = 5x$. Explain how you would model the equation. How is it similar to the two-step equations you have modeled in the lesson? How is it different? Use 3 positive variable tiles and two +1-tiles on the left. Use 5 positive variable tiles on the right. Both types use algebra tiles to model but for this one, there are variable tiles, rather than constant tiles, on both sides. **DOK 3; MP.4**

GETTING READY FOR GRADE 7

GR4.3 Writing Two-Step Equations

Engage

ESSENTIAL QUESTION

How do you write two-step equations? Choose a variable for what you are trying to find. Put the numbers and variable together with math operations to write an equation that shows the relationships in the problem.

Motivate the Lesson

Ask: How do you combine two operations, such as multiplying and adding, into an equation that describes a situation? Begin the Explore Activity to find out.

Explore

EXPLORE ACTIVITY Connect Vocabulary ELL

Help students connect the math word *variable* with the answer to the question "what are you trying to find?" Have students look for the question in the problem, and predict the form of the answer, for example, "so many weeks" or "so many miles."

Questioning Strategies

- What are some other ways you could write the final equation? Sample answers: $85 = 30 + 6w$ or $6w + 30 = 85$
- What operation does $6w$ indicate? Multiply the factors 6 and w

Explain

YOUR TURN Avoid Common Errors

Exercise 1 Some students may write incorrectly the relationship "each color of ribbon cost \$8, how many colors of ribbon did she buy?" because they try to add \$8. Suggest that they begin by writing "Each color of ribbon costs \$8" as 8r. Then ask them to think about how they could represent the ribbon and the book equals \$34, the amount Hannah spent.

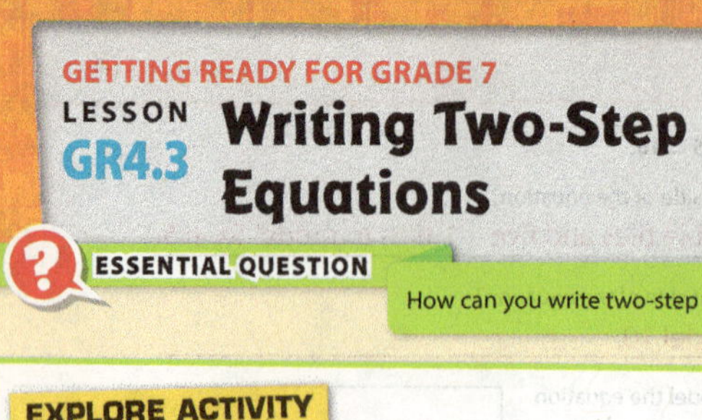

GETTING READY FOR GRADE 7

LESSON GR4.3 **Writing Two-Step Equations**

ESSENTIAL QUESTION

How can you write two-step equations?

EXPLORE ACTIVITY

A two-step equation uses two operations. You can use numbers, variables, and operations to write two-step equations for real-world problems.

Jamie wants to buy a guitar that costs \$85. He already has \$30 and plans to save \$6 a week to buy the guitar. How many weeks will it take him to save enough money to buy the guitar? Write an equation that will help Jamie find how many weeks it will take him to save the money.

A Identify what you need to find to solve the problem. This will be the variable in the equation.

Which phrase identifies the variable? how many weeks

Let w represent the number of weeks it will take Jamie to save the money.

B Identify numbers and operations that you can use to write an equation.

amount Jamie already has: \$30

amount Jamie can save each week: \$6

amount Jamie will save in w weeks: \$6w

cost of the guitar: \$85

C Use the information to write an equation.

amount Jamie has	plus	6	times	weeks of saving	equals	cost of guitar
↓	↓	↓	↓	↓	↓	↓
30	+	6	•	w	=	85

So, the equation $30 + 6w = 85$ can help Jamie find how many weeks it will take him to save the money.

Getting Ready Lesson 4.3 42

ADDITIONAL PRACTICE

1. Sydney buys 4 tomato plants and a \$6 pepper plant for a total of \$18. Write an equation to find the cost of each tomato plant. $4p + 6 = 18$
2. Gail borrows \$275 to buy a bicycle. She pays back \$50 the first week and \$25 each week until her debt is paid off. Write an equation to find how many more weeks, after the first week, it will be until she has repaid the loan. $\$275 = 50 + 25w$
3. Harry wants to eat a 650-calorie meal. He eats one sandwich of 554 calories and some pickles of 12 calories each. Write an equation to find how many pickles he can eat. $650 = 554 + 12p$
4. Kyle reads 20 pages each day. He has read 114 pages of a 254-page book. Write an equation to find how many days it will take him to finish the book. $20d + 114 = 254$

YOUR TURN

Write a two-step equation to solve the problem. Let r represent the number of ribbon colors.

1. Hannah spent \$34 on a book and some ribbon. If the book cost \$10 and each color of ribbon cost \$8, how many colors of ribbon did she buy? $8r + 10 = 34$

Guided Practice

1. Jill sold half of her comic books and then bought 16 more. She now has 36. How many comic books did she have in the beginning?

   Let c represent the beginning number of comic books Jill had.

   What is the important information from the problem?

   number of comic books sold: $\frac{1}{2}c$ final number of comic books: 36

   number of comic books bought: 16

   What is the two-step equation that can be used to find the beginning number of comic books? $\frac{1}{2}c + 16 = 36$

ESSENTIAL QUESTION CHECK-IN

2. How can you use the information in a problem to write a two-step equation? Sample answer: Identify a variable to represent what you need to find. Then identify the important information that tells you what numbers and operations to use to write the equation.

Independent Practice

Write a two-step equation to solve each problem.

3. The total cost of 12 soccer uniforms with an \$8 shipping fee is \$248. Write an equation you can use to find the cost of each uniform. Let c represent the cost of a soccer uniform. $12c + 8 = 248$

4. Christine had \$28 to spend on eight avocados. After buying them she had \$4. How much did each avocado cost? Let a represent the cost of an avocado. $8a + 4 = 28$

5. Write a real-world problem that could be represented by the equation $3x + 16 = 22$. Sample answer: Shaun had \$22 to spend on three notebooks. After buying them he had \$16. How much did each notebook cost?

Elaborate

Talk About It **Summarize the Lesson**

Ask: What is needed to write a two-step equation? Analyze what the problem is asking for. This will be the variable. Identify important information in the problem, and use the words in the equation to tie the information together mathematically.

GUIDED PRACTICE **Avoid Common Errors**

Exercise 1 Some students may try to begin by translating the first sentence. Tell students to first read the entire problem and analyze what the problem is asking for. Then identify a variable that will answer the question.

Evaluate

LESSON QUIZ

1. A waiter earns \$32 in tips, plus his hourly wage, for working 6 hours. He earns a total of \$74. Write an equation to find his hourly wage. $6w + 32 = 74$

2. Jean mows 16 lawns in March. That is 2 fewer than three times as many as in February. Write an equation to find the number of lawns mowed in February. $16 = 3f - 2$

3. The cost of a pizza is \$8.85 plus \$0.50 for each extra topping. The total cost for Alex's pizza is \$10.35. Write an equation to find how many extra toppings Alex chose. $10.35 = 8.85 + 0.50t$

4. Laura pays a total of \$38.45 to rent a car for a day. The company charges \$35 a day plus \$0.15 per mile. Write an equation to find how many miles Laura drove. $38.45 = 35 + 0.15m$

H.O.T. FOCUS ON HIGHER ORDER THINKING

1. **Multiple Representations** Describe a situation and ask a question that could be answered by using the equation $\$10 + \$8w = \$120$. Sample answer: Jen deposits \$10 in a savings account and adds \$8 each week until she has \$120. How many weeks did she take to save this much? **DOK 2; MP.3**

2. **Analyze Relationships** How can you tell if an equation is a two-step equation or a one-step equation? Look at the number of operations. For example, a one-step equation might have only multiplication while a two-step equation might have multiplication and addition. **DOK 3; MP.7**

GETTING READY FOR GRADE 7

GR4.4 Solving Two-Step Equations

Engage

ESSENTIAL QUESTION

How do you solve two-step equations? Use a model to represent the problem. Then use inverse operations to first undo addition or subtraction then undo multiplication or division to both sides of the equation until the variable is by itself.

Motivate the Lesson

Ask: Remember when you used the Order of Operations to multiply before you add or subtract? How can you reverse this process to undo operations? Begin the Explore Activity to find out.

Explore

EXPLORE ACTIVITY Questioning Strategies

- What has been done to the variable *x* in the original equation? It has been multiplied by 2 and 3 has been subtracted.
- Which operation will you undo first to reverse this? First, undo the subtraction by adding +3 to each side of the equation.

Explain

YOUR TURN Avoid Common Errors

Exercise 2 Some students may incorrectly try to begin by dividing the variable tiles into 3 equal groups. Remind them that the +1, or addition operation, is undone first (reversing the order of operations).

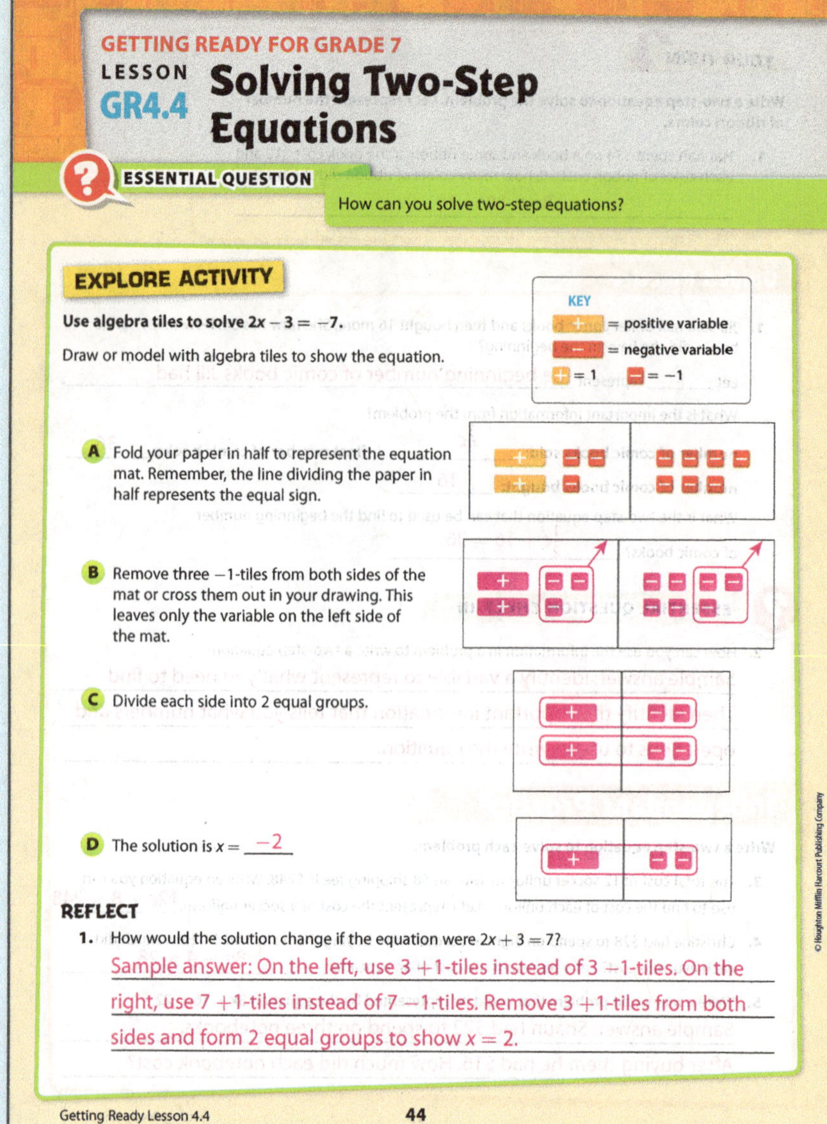

ADDITIONAL PRACTICE

Solve each equation. If needed, use or draw algebra tiles to model each equation.

1. $4p + 6 = 18$ $p = 3$
2. $3x - 2 = 10$ $x = 4$
3. $5y - 7 = 23$ $y = 6$
4. $6n + 6 = 12$ $n = 1$
5. $7a + 3 = 17$ $a = 2$
6. $2b - 10 = 14$ $b = 12$
7. $8w - 5 = 27$ $w = 4$
8. $5x + 1 = 16$ $x = 3$
9. $10p - 2 = 18$ $p = 2$
10. $9y + 6 = 42$ $y = 4$

YOUR TURN

Use or draw algebra tiles to model and solve each equation.

2. $3n + 1 = 13$ $n = 4$ **3.** $2x - 4 = -10$ $x = -3$ **4.** $2y + 1 = 5$ $y = 2$

Guided Practice

Tell how to solve the equation for x.

1. What equation do the algebra tiles model? $3x + 2 = 14$

What is the first step in solving the equation? Remove 2 +1-tiles from each side of the equation.

What is the second step in solving the equation? Divide each side into 3 equal groups.

What is the solution? $x = 4$

ESSENTIAL QUESTION CHECK-IN

2. How can algebra tiles or drawings help you solve a two-step equation? Sample answer: They help show how to leave only the variable on one side and how to make equal groups to find the value of the variable.

Independent Practice

Solve the equation.

3. $4x - 2 = -6$ $x = -1$ **4.** $5w + 3 = 13$ $w = 2$ **5.** $2y + 4 = 10$ $y = 3$

6. $3n - 1 = -10$ $n = -3$ **7.** $6x + 7 = 13$ $x = 1$ **8.** $3a - 2 = -8$ $a = -2$

9. Jason has 11 model cars. He has one more than twice as many model cars as he has model planes. Write a two-step equation to find how many model planes Jason has. Then solve the equation. $2m + 1 = 11; m = 5$

H.O.T. FOCUS ON HIGHER ORDER THINKING

1. **Multi-step** Use the equation $16 = 3f - 2$. **DOK 3; MP.3**

a. Why is the first step in solving the equation to add 2? Adding 2 is the inverse operation for subtracting 2.

b. Why must you do the same operation on both sides of the equation? To keep the rewritten equation equivalent to the original equation.

c. What is the second step in solving this equation? Divide both sides by 3.

d. How do you choose the operation in the second step? Since the variable is multiplied by 3, you do the inverse operation, dividing by 3, in order to isolate the variable.

Elaborate

Talk About It

Summarize the Lesson

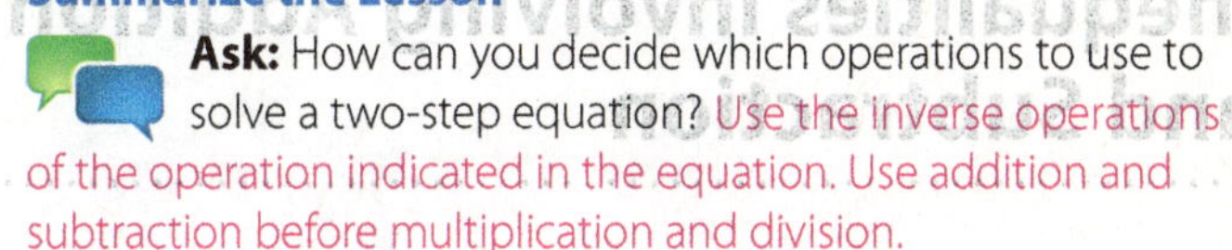

Ask: How can you decide which operations to use to solve a two-step equation? Use the inverse operations of the operation indicated in the equation. Use addition and subtraction before multiplication and division.

Focus on Math Connections **Mathematical Processes and Practices**

Discuss how the order of solving a two-step equation relates to the order of operations used to simplify an expression. Show how the equation solving operations are performed in the *reverse* order of the order of operations. So, students solve a two-step equation by first adding or subtracting and then multiplying or dividing.

GUIDED PRACTICE

Talk About It

Check for Understanding

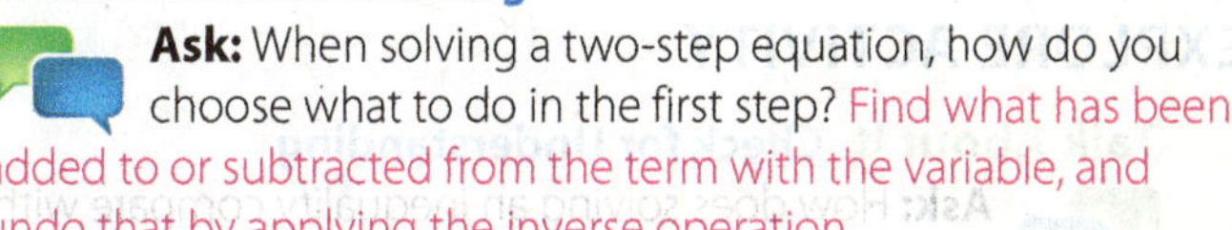

Ask: When solving a two-step equation, how do you choose what to do in the first step? Find what has been added to or subtracted from the term with the variable, and undo that by applying the inverse operation.

In Exercise 1, what do you do after you have divided each side into 3 equal groups? Divide by 3 (the inverse of multiplying by 3) by keeping just 1 group out of the 3 groups on each side.

Evaluate

LESSON QUIZ

Solve the equation.

1. $5b - 8 = 17$ $b = 5$ **2.** $9a + 3 = 21$ $a = 2$

3. $7x - 6 = 36$ $x = 6$ **4.** $4y + 4 = 36$ $y = 8$

GETTING READY FOR GRADE 7

GR4.5 Solving One-Step Inequalities Involving Addition and Subtraction

Engage

ESSENTIAL QUESTION

How do you solve inequalities involving addition and subtraction? Use the properties of inequality involving addition and subtraction and inverse operations to isolate the variable.

Motivate the Lesson

Ask: How does what you know about solving an equation help you to solve an inequality? Begin the Explore Activity to find out.

Explore

EXPLORE ACTIVITY

Talk About It Check for Understanding

Ask: How does solving an inequality compare with solving an equation? What is alike and what is different? For equations and inequalities, you isolate the variable by adding or subtracting numbers to both sides. The solution to an equation is one number value for the variable. The solution to an inequality is a range of many number values for the variable.

Explain

YOUR TURN Avoid Common Errors

Exercise 1 Some students may incorrectly show a closed circle to graph the solution. Review the fact that $n < -5$ means that $n = -5$ is not included in the solution set.

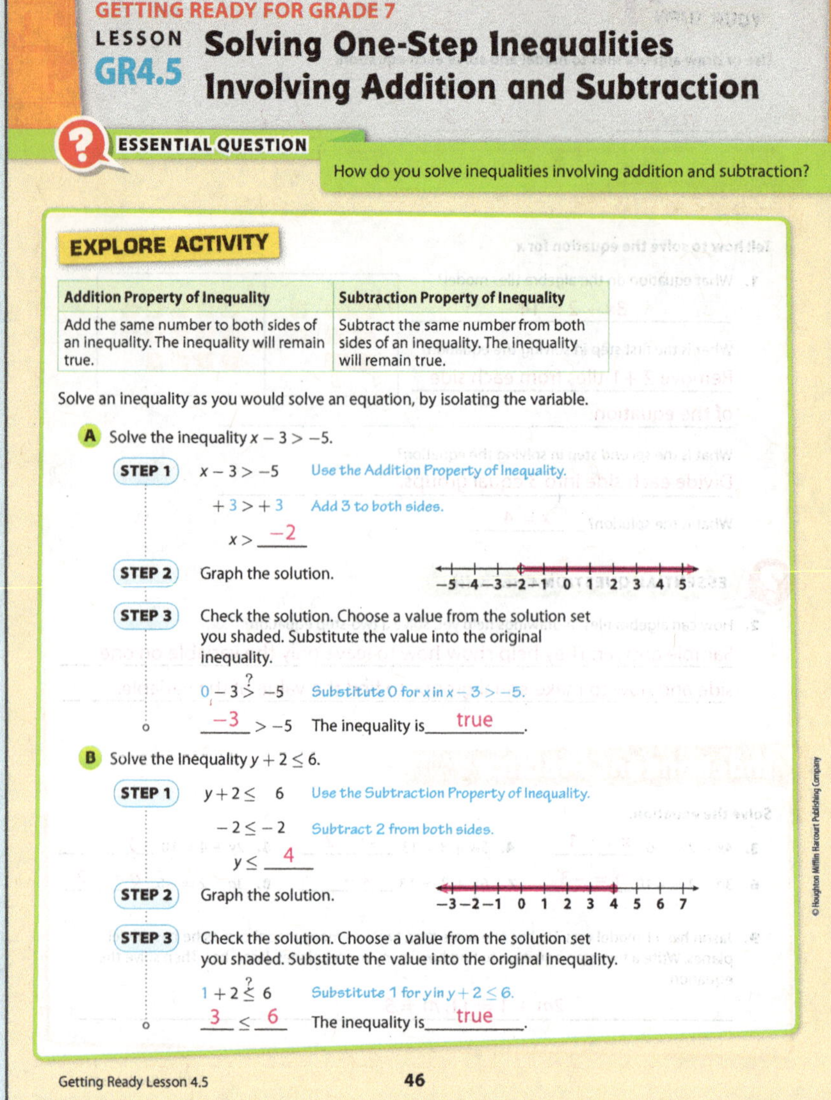

GETTING READY FOR GRADE 7

LESSON GR4.5 **Solving One-Step Inequalities Involving Addition and Subtraction**

ESSENTIAL QUESTION

How do you solve inequalities involving addition and subtraction?

EXPLORE ACTIVITY

Addition Property of Inequality	Subtraction Property of Inequality
Add the same number to both sides of an inequality. The inequality will remain true.	Subtract the same number from both sides of an inequality. The inequality will remain true.

Solve an inequality as you would solve an equation, by isolating the variable.

A Solve the inequality $x - 3 > -5$.

STEP 1 $x - 3 > -5$ Use the Addition Property of Inequality.

$+3 > +3$ Add 3 to both sides.

$x >$ __−2__

STEP 2 Graph the solution.

STEP 3 Check the solution. Choose a value from the solution set you shaded. Substitute the value into the original inequality.

$0 - 3 \overset{?}{>} -5$ Substitute 0 for x in $x - 3 > -5$.

__−3__ > -5 The inequality is __true__.

B Solve the inequality $y + 2 \le 6$.

STEP 1 $y + 2 \le 6$ Use the Subtraction Property of Inequality.

$-2 \le -2$ Subtract 2 from both sides.

$y \le$ __4__

STEP 2 Graph the solution.

STEP 3 Check the solution. Choose a value from the solution set you shaded. Substitute the value into the original inequality.

$1 + 2 \overset{?}{\le} 6$ Substitute 1 for y in $y + 2 \le 6$.

__3__ $\le$ __6__ The inequality is __true__.

ADDITIONAL PRACTICE

Solve each inequality and answer the questions for each.

1. $x + 3 < 0$ $x < -3$
   a. Does the graph begin with a closed circle? no
   b. Does the arrow go to the left? yes
   c. Is the value −5 included in the solution set? yes
   d. Is the value −2 included in the solution set? no
2. $p - 1 \ge 0$ $p \ge 1$
   a. Does the graph begin with a closed circle? yes
   b. Does the arrow go to the left? no
   c. Is the value 2 included in the solution set? yes
   d. Is the value −1 included in the solution set? no

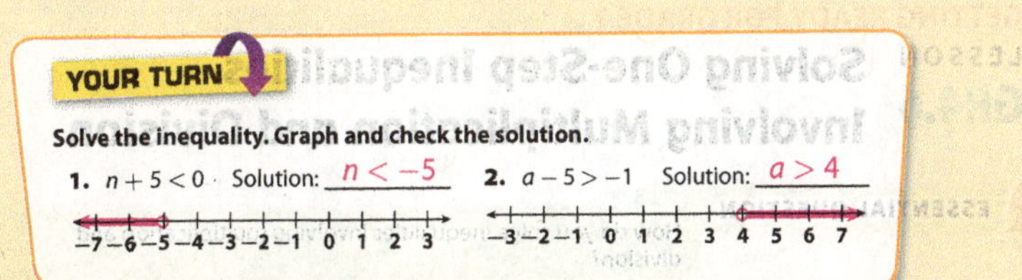

Guided Practice

Solve the inequality. Graph and check the solution.

1. $y - 2 \geq -1$
   $+2 \geq +2$
   $y \geq 1$

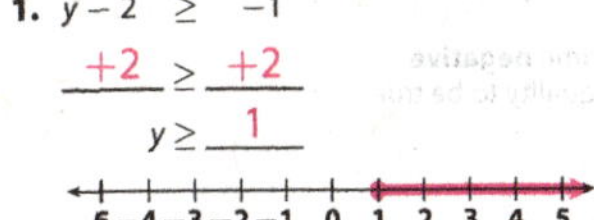

2. $x + 4 < 2$
   $-4 < -4$
   $x < -2$

ESSENTIAL QUESTION CHECK-IN

3. How do you know which property of inequality to use to solve an addition or subtraction inequality?
   Use the property for the operation that will isolate the variable.

Independent Practice

Solve each inequality. Graph and check the solution.

4. $n + 8 > 5$ $n > -3$

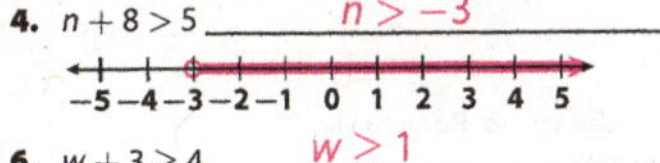

5. $c - 2 \leq -6$ $c \leq -4$

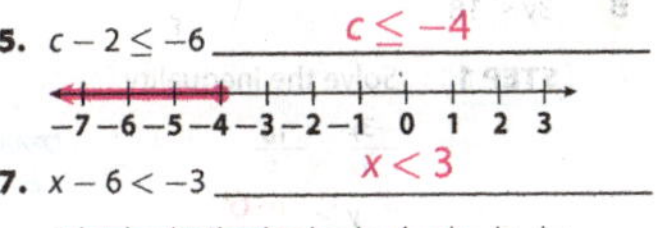

6. $w + 3 \geq 4$ $w \geq 1$
7. $x - 6 < -3$ $x < 3$
8. Clara wants to have more than $8 to take to the museum. She has $5. How much more money does she need? Write an inequality to represent the problem. Then solve the problem.
   Let m = the money Clara needs; $m + 5 > 8$; $m > 3$; Clara needs more than $3.

H.O.T. FOCUS ON HIGHER ORDER THINKING

1. **Analyze Relaionthips**
   a. Solve the inequality $x - 3 < 2$. $x < 5$
   b. Solve the inequality $2 > x - 3$. $5 > x$
   c. What conclusion can you draw about these two inequalities? They have the same solution set and are equivalent inequalities.
   d. Which form of this inequality do you find easier to read and work with? Answers will vary; some students find it less confusing to keep the variable always on the left. **DOK 3; MP.3**

Elaborate

Talk About It

Summarize the Lesson

Ask: How do you solve an equality involving addition and subtraction? Use the properties of inequality and inverse operations to isolate the variable. Graph the solution on a number line to check.

GUIDED PRACTICE

Avoid Common Errors

Exercise 1 Some students may begin their graph with an open circle. Remind them that ≤ and ≥ mean that the starting value IS included, so the circle must be a closed one.

Talk About It

Check for Understanding

Ask: How do you check the solution to an inequality? Choose one point that is on your graph and substitute it in the original inequality to see if the sample value makes the inequality true. You can also choose a point that is not on your graph and substitute it to see if it makes the inequality false.

Evaluate

LESSON QUIZ

Solve the inequality. Graph and check the solution.

1. $x + 3 > 7$ $x > 4$

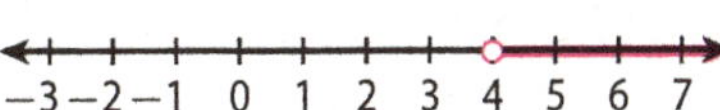

2. $a + 1 > -1$ $a > -2$

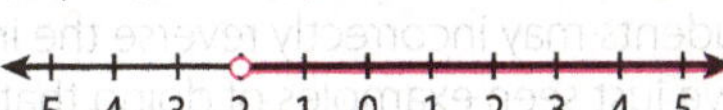

3. $p + 5 \leq 1$ $p \leq -4$

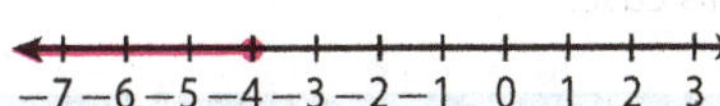

GETTING READY FOR GRADE 7

GR4.6 Solving One-Step Inequalities Involving Multiplication and Division

Engage

ESSENTIAL QUESTION

How do you solve inequalities involving multiplication and division? Use the properties of Inequality involving multiplication and division and use inverse operations to isolate the variable.

Motivate the Lesson

Ask: How can you use what you know about solving inequalities with addition and subtraction help you with solving inequalities with multiplication and division? Begin the Explore Activity to find out.

Explore

EXPLORE ACTIVITY Engage with the Whiteboard

In Explore Activity Part B, have students draw the graph and then test these points to see whether or not they make the inequality true or false: −8, −6, −2, 0. Lead students to see that the point −8 does not belong on the graph because it makes the inequality false; all the others are on the graph and make the inequality true.

Explain

YOUR TURN Avoid Common Errors

Exercise 1 Some students may incorrectly reverse the inequality sign because they have just seen examples of doing that. Ask students to describe the special conditions that reverse the sign, and to verify that you do *not* need to divide or multiply by a negative number in this case.

GETTING READY FOR GRADE 7

LESSON GR4.6 **Solving One-Step Inequalities Involving Multiplication and Division**

ESSENTIAL QUESTION

How do you solve inequalities involving multiplication and division?

EXPLORE ACTIVITY

Multiplication and Division Properties of Inequality

- If you multiply or divide both sides of an inequality by the same **positive** number, the inequality will remain true.
- If you multiply or divide both sides of an inequality by the same **negative** number, you must reverse the inequality symbol for the inequality to be true.

Solve each inequality. Graph and check the solution.

A $\frac{x}{4} > 2$

STEP 1 Solve the inequality.

$4\left(\frac{x}{4}\right) > 4(2)$ Multiply both sides by 4.

$x >$ 8

STEP 2 Graph the solution.

STEP 3 Check the solution.

$\frac{12}{4} \overset{?}{>} 2$ Substitute 12 for *x* in $\frac{x}{4} > 2$.

3 > 2 The inequality is true.

B $-3y \le 18$

STEP 1 Solve the inequality.

$\frac{-3y}{-3} \ge \frac{18}{-3}$ Divide both sides by −3. Reverse the inequality symbol.

$y \ge$ −6

STEP 2 Graph the solution.

STEP 3 Check the solution.

$-3(-4) \overset{?}{\le} 18$ Substitute −4 for *y* in $-3y \le 18$.

$12 \le 18$ The inequality is true

Getting Ready Lesson 4.6 48

© Houghton Mifflin Harcourt Publishing Company

ADDITIONAL PRACTICE

Solve each inequality. Graph and check the solution.

1. $-3x > -6$ $x < 2$

2. $-2y \le -12$ $y \ge 6$

3. $\frac{1}{4}n \le -4$ $n \le -16$

4. $\frac{p}{-2} < -4$ $p > 8$

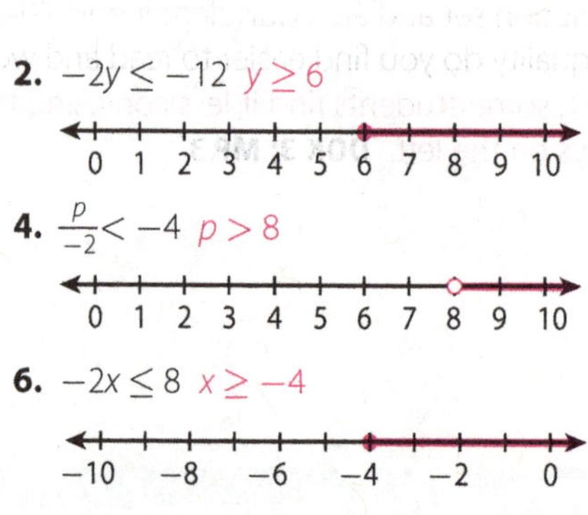

5. $-4x > 12$ $x < -3$

6. $-2x \le 8$ $x \ge -4$

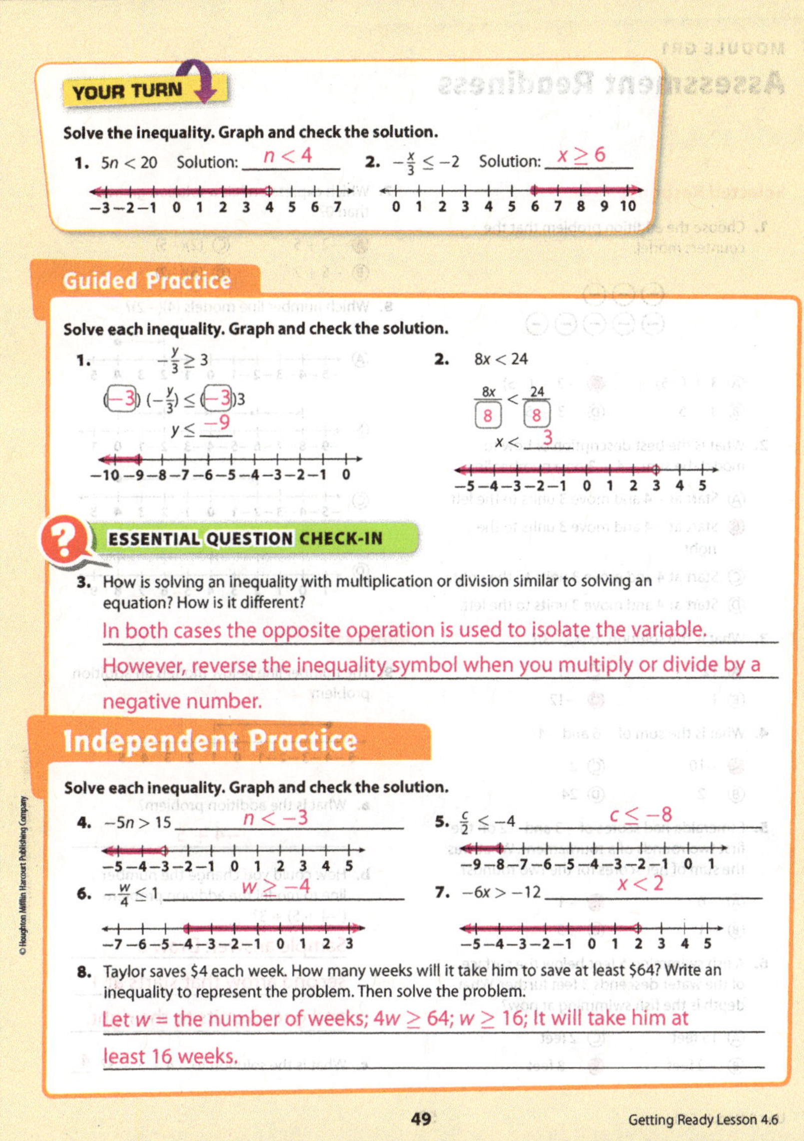

YOUR TURN

Solve the inequality. Graph and check the solution.

1. $5n < 20$ Solution: $n < 4$
2. $-\frac{x}{3} \leq -2$ Solution: $x \geq 6$

Guided Practice

Solve each inequality. Graph and check the solution.

1. $-\frac{y}{3} \geq 3$

   $(-3)(-\frac{y}{3}) \leq (-3)3$

   $y \leq -9$

2. $8x < 24$

   $\frac{8x}{8} < \frac{24}{8}$

   $x < 3$

ESSENTIAL QUESTION CHECK-IN

3. How is solving an inequality with multiplication or division similar to solving an equation? How is it different?
   In both cases the opposite operation is used to isolate the variable. However, reverse the inequality symbol when you multiply or divide by a negative number.

Independent Practice

Solve each inequality. Graph and check the solution.

4. $-5n > 15$ $n < -3$
5. $\frac{c}{2} \leq -4$ $c \leq -8$
6. $-\frac{w}{4} \leq 1$ $w \geq -4$
7. $-6x > -12$ $x < 2$
8. Taylor saves \$4 each week. How many weeks will it take him to save at least \$64? Write an inequality to represent the problem. Then solve the problem.
   Let w = the number of weeks; $4w \geq 64$; $w \geq 16$; It will take him at least 16 weeks.

49 Getting Ready Lesson 4.6

FOCUS ON HIGHER ORDER THINKING

1. **Analyze Relationships** Does adding or subtracting the same number on both sides of an inequality change the direction of the inequality? Does multiplying or dividing by a positive number change the direction of the inequality? What does change the direction of the inequality? No; No; Multiplying or dividing by a negative number. **DOK 3; MP.4**

2. **Justify Reasoning** Before solving an inequality, can you look at its symbol and tell which way the arrow on the graph will point? Explain. No, you can't be sure that the inequality sign won't need to be reversed until you solve it. **DOK 3; MP.7**

Elaborate

Talk About It **Summarize the Lesson**

Ask: How do you solve an inequality involving multiplication or division? Use the properties of Inequality involving multiplication and division and use inverse operations to isolate the variable.

Avoid Common Errors

Exercise 5 Some students may incorrectly reverse the inequality sign because they see the −8. Ask them if they multiplied or divided both sides by a negative number. Additionally, some students may not see how to use inverse operations in this problem. Ask: What has been done to *c*? Then ask: What inverse operation can you use to undo that operation?

Talk About It **Check for Understanding**

Ask: How do you check the solution to an inequality? Choose one point that is on your graph and substitute it in the original inequality to see if the sample value makes the inequality true. You can also choose a point that is *not* on your graph and substitute it to see if it makes the inequality false.

Evaluate

LESSON QUIZ

Solve the inequality. Graph and check the solution.

1. $\frac{y}{-2} \leq 3$ $y \geq -6$

   −10 −8 −6 −4 −2 0

2. $-\frac{1}{3}a > -1$ $a < 3$

   −5 −4 −3 −2 −1 0 1 2 3 4 5

3. $3x < 12$ $x < 4$

   −3 −2 −1 0 1 2 3 4 5 6 7

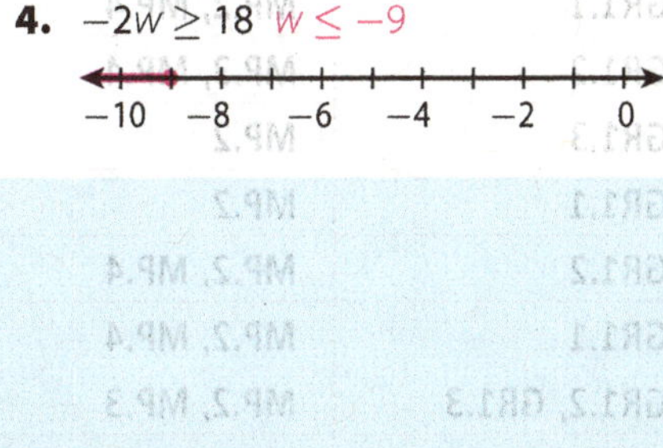

4. $-2w \geq 18$ $w \leq -9$

   −10 −8 −6 −4 −2 0

Assessment Readiness

Assessment Readiness Tip Students can create a model to match the problem situation.

Item 2 If students create a horizontal number line and try the movement described in each answer choice, they can see which choice best models the correct movement.

Item 6 Students can create their own vertical number line to more easily track the movement in this problem, drawing the surface of the water at 0.

Avoid Common Errors

Item 4 Students may subtract the numbers when taking the sum, confused by the presence of negative signs. Remind students that when finding the sum of two addends with the same sign, add them and keep the sign. Only when there are two different signs (a negative and a positive) should they subtract the numbers.

Item 9 Some students may translate the number line as meaning $-4 + 1$. Remind them that the second addend is represented by the length and direction of the arrow, not the endpoint of the arrow.

MODULE GR1

Assessment Readiness

Selected Response

1. Choose the addition problem that the counters model.

Ⓐ $3 + (-5)$ **Ⓒ $-3 + (-5)$**
Ⓑ $3 - 5$ Ⓓ $-3 + 5$

2. What is the best description of how to model the sum $-4 + 3$ on a number line?

Ⓐ Start at -4 and move 3 units to the left.
Ⓑ Start at -4 and move 3 units to the right.
Ⓒ Start at 4 and move 3 units to the right.
Ⓓ Start at 4 and move 3 units to the left.

3. What is the solution to $(4)(-3)$?

Ⓐ 12 Ⓒ -1
Ⓑ 1 **Ⓓ -12**

4. What is the sum of -6 and -4?

Ⓐ -10 Ⓒ 2
Ⓑ -2 Ⓓ 24

5. Esmeralda had scores of $+3$ and -2 on the first two rounds of a tournament. What was the sum of her scores for the two rounds?

Ⓐ -6 **Ⓒ $+1$**
Ⓑ -1 Ⓓ $+5$

6. A fish swimming 5 feet below the surface of the water descends 3 feet further. What depth is the fish swimming at now?

Ⓐ 15 feet Ⓒ 2 feet
Ⓑ -2 feet **Ⓓ -8 feet**

7. Which expression has a solution greater than 0?

Ⓐ $-2 + 5$ Ⓒ $(2)(-5)$
Ⓑ $-5 + 2$ Ⓓ $(5)(-2)$

8. Which number line models $(4)(-2)$?

Ⓐ 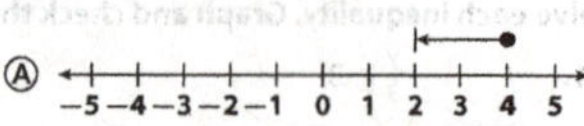

Ⓑ 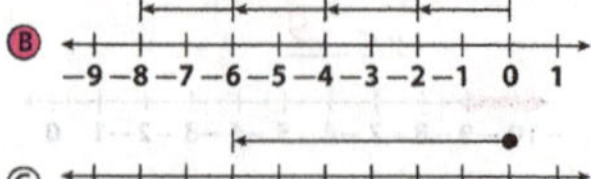

Ⓒ −5 −4 −3 −2 −1 0 1 2 3 4 5

Ⓓ 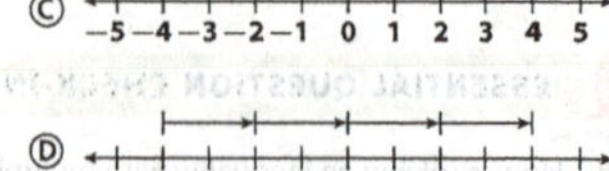

Mini-Task

9. The number line below models an addition problem.

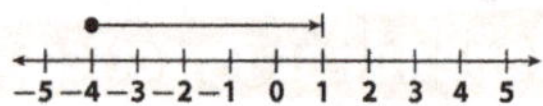

a. What is the addition problem? $-4 + 5$

b. How could you change the number line to model the addition problem $(-4 + 5) + 3$?

Sample answer: Draw a second arrow that starts at 1 and goes 3 units to the right.

c. What is the solution to $-4 + 5 + 3$? 4

Items	Lesson	Mathematical Processes and Practices
1	GR1.1	MP.2, MP.4
2	GR1.2	MP.3, MP.4
3	GR1.3	MP.2
4	GR1.1	MP.2
5	GR1.2	MP.2, MP.4
6	GR1.1	MP.2, MP.4
7	GR1.2, GR1.3	MP.2, MP.3
8	GR1.3	MP.1, MP.2, MP.3, MP.4
9	GR1.2	MP.1, MP.2, MP.3, MP.4

MODULE GR2

Assessment Readiness

Selected Response

1. Which ratio is equivalent to $\frac{2}{3}$?

   (A) $\frac{3}{4}$ (B) $\frac{4}{6}$ (C) $\frac{4}{9}$ (D) $\frac{3}{2}$

2. What is the sum of 2.5 and −1.5?

   (A) −4 (B) −1 (C) 1 (D) 4

3. Which fraction is equivalent to $-\frac{5}{4}$?

   (A) $-\frac{4}{5}$ (B) $\frac{-5}{-4}$ (C) $\frac{-4}{-5}$ (D) $\frac{5}{-4}$

4. What is the product of (3)(−4.5)?

   (A) 7.5 (B) 1.5 (C) −1.5 (D) −13.5

5. Which expression is modeled on the number line shown?

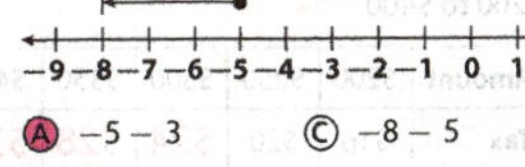

   (A) −5 − 3 (B) −5 + 3 (C) −8 − 5 (D) −8 − 3

6. What is the difference of 2 − 4?

   (A) 2 (B) −2 (C) −3 (D) −7

7. Aaron bought two blocks of cheese. One weighed 1.25 lb and the other weighed 2.5 lb. What was the total weight of the cheese?

   (A) 1 lb (B) 1.25 lb (C) 3.5 lb (D) 3.75 lb

8. A recipe uses 1 cup of lemon juice to make 6 glasses of lemonade. Maria wants to make enough lemonade for 24 glasses. How many cups of lemon juice does she need?

   (A) 4 cups (B) 6 cups (C) 19 cups (D) 24 cups

9. What is the quotient of 40 and (−4)?

   (A) 44 (B) 36 (C) 10 (D) −10

10. Tim went to the store with $6.25. The groceries he wanted cost $4.75 in all. How much money does Tim have left over?

    (A) $1.50 (B) $1.75 (C) $2.50 (D) $2.75

Mini-Task

11. Sometimes you can tell the sign of a sum or product without solving.

    a. The sum of 4.25 and −3.75 must be positive. How can you tell without solving?

    Sample answer: On a number line, 4.25 is further to the right of 0 than −3.75 is to the left of 0. So, their sum is positive.

    b. The product of 4.25 and −3.75 must be negative. How can you tell without solving?

    Sample answer: 4.25 and −3.75 have different signs. So, their product must be negative.

Assessment Readiness

Assessment Readiness Tip Students can use a chart to remember the sign of a solution to a multiplication or division problem with integers.

Item 4 Students can use a chart to decide the sign of the answer. Fill in the chart as shown below, with positive signs on a diagonal and negative signs everywhere else. Since this item is a positive number multiplied by a negative number, use the top row, which shows that a positive times a negative is a negative:

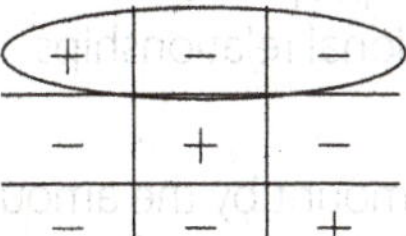

Item 9 Using the same chart, students can see that a positive number divided by a negative number is negative by looking at the top row.

Avoid Common Errors

Item 1 Students sometimes believe that the order in a ratio does not matter. Remind students that order does matter, and $\frac{3}{2} \neq \frac{2}{3}$. Therefore these ratios are not equivalent.

Item 3 Students are most used to seeing a negative sign either in the numerator of a fraction or in front of a fraction. Remind students that when a negative sign is in the denominator, it means the same thing as in the other two positions.

Items	Lesson	Mathematical Processes and Practices
1	GR2.1	MP.2
2	GR2.2	MP.2
3	GR2.5	MP.2, MP.6, MP.8
4	GR2.4	MP.2
5	GR2.3	MP.2, MP.4
6	GR2.3	MP.2
7	GR2.2	MP.2
8	GR2.1	MP.2
9	GR2.5	MP.2
10	GR2.3	MP.2
11	GR2.2, GR2.4	MP.1, MP.2, MP.3, MP.8

Assessment Readiness

Assessment Readiness Tip Using formulas is the most efficient and accurate way to solve interest problems.

Item 6 Some students may have difficulty when converting a percent to a decimal. Remind students that percent means per hundred. For example, $7\% = 7 \times 0.01 = 0.07$.

Avoid Common Errors

Item 2 Some students may see any straight-line graph and mistakenly assume that it has to represent a proportional relationship. Remind students that proportional relationships *must* pass through the origin.

Item 7 Students may divide the original amount by the amount of change. Remind students the amount of change should be divided by the original amount. If the change is greater than the original amount, it is a percent increase. If the change is less than the original amount, it is a percent decrease.

MODULE GR3

Assessment Readiness

Selected Response

1. A bicyclist rode 32 miles in two hours. What is the bicyclist's unit rate?
   - Ⓐ 32 miles per hour
   - Ⓑ 30 miles per hour
   - Ⓒ 16 miles per hour
   - Ⓓ $\frac{2}{32}$ miles per hour
2. Which graph shows a proportional relationship?

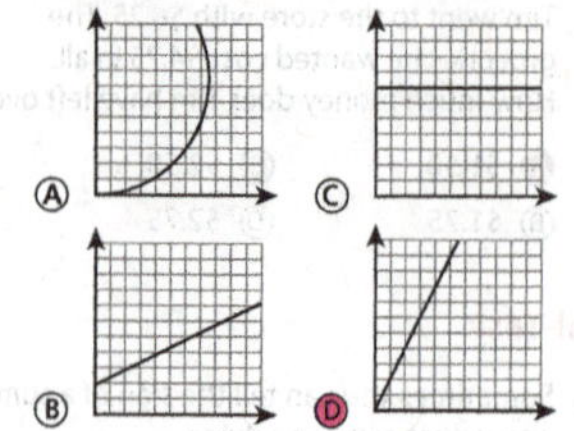

3. What is 20% of 1,500?
   - Ⓐ 300
   - Ⓑ 200
   - Ⓒ 30
   - Ⓓ 20
4. The table shows a worker's earnings based on the number of hours worked. Which amount completes the table correctly?

Hours	1	2	3	4
Earnings	$15	$30		$60

   - Ⓐ $31
   - Ⓑ $35
   - Ⓒ $40
   - Ⓓ $45
5. The population of a town rose from 300 to 330 over two years. What was the percent increase in population?
   - Ⓐ 5%
   - Ⓑ 10%
   - Ⓒ 30%
   - Ⓓ 110%
6. Eun borrows $2,500 for six years. She is charged 4% simple interest per year. How much interest will she pay over the six years?
   - Ⓐ $3,100
   - Ⓑ $2,600
   - Ⓒ $600
   - Ⓓ $100
7. What is the percent change from 40 to 50?
   - Ⓐ 20% increase
   - Ⓑ 25% increase
   - Ⓒ 20% decrease
   - Ⓓ 25% decrease
8. A pair of binoculars costs $45. Sales tax adds 6% to the cost. What do the binoculars cost, including sales tax?
   - Ⓐ $45.06
   - Ⓑ $47.40
   - Ⓒ $47.70
   - Ⓓ $51.00

Mini-Task

9. The table below is used to find the state sales tax due on purchases ranging from $200 to $400.

Amount	$200	$250	$300	$350	$400
Tax	$16	$20	$24	$28	$32

   a. Circle the sales tax rate.

   4% 8% 10%

   b. Complete the missing entries in the table.

   c. Explain how you can tell whether the table shows a proportional relationship.

   Sample answer: If the rate of change is constant from ratio of tax to amount in each column, the relationship is proportional.

Unit 8 Module GR3 52

Items	Lesson	Mathematical Processes and Practices
1	GR3.1	MP.2
2	GR3.3	MP.2, MP.4
3	GR3.4	MP.2
4	GR3.2	MP.2, MP.4, MP.7
5	GR3.5	MP.1, MP.2
6	GR3.6	MP.2, MP.5
7	GR3.5	MP.2
8	GR3.4	MP.1, MP.2, MP.5
9	GR3.2, GR3.4, GR3.6	MP.1, MP.2, MP.4, MP.7, MP.8

MODULE GR4

Assessment Readiness

Selected Response

1. Which number line shows the solution to $x + 2 > 5$?

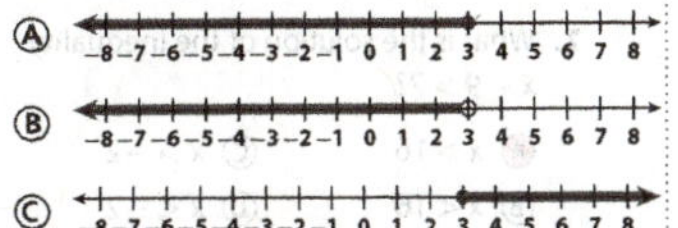

Ⓐ Ⓑ Ⓒ Ⓓ

2. Which factored algebraic expression is modeled by the tiles shown?

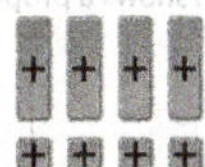

Ⓐ $4(x + 1)$ Ⓒ $4(x + 2)$
Ⓑ $2(2x + 1)$ Ⓓ $2(x + 4)$

3. It cost \$24 per car plus \$8 per passenger to ride on a ferry. Helene paid \$64 when she drove her car onto the ferry. Which equation could be used to find p, the number of passengers in Helene's car?

Ⓐ $8p = 64$ Ⓒ $32p = 64$
Ⓑ $8p + 24 = 64$ Ⓓ $24p + 8 = 64$

4. Which equation is modeled by the tiles shown?

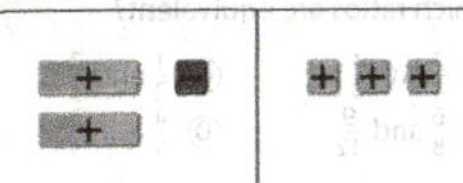

Ⓐ $2x + 1 = 3$ Ⓒ $2x - 3 = 1$
Ⓑ $2x - 1 = 3$ Ⓓ $2x + 3 = 1$

5. What is the solution to the inequality $3x < 12$?

Ⓐ $x < 9$ Ⓒ $x < 4$
Ⓑ $x > 9$ Ⓓ $x > 4$

6. The algebra tiles shown model the equation $4x + 3 = 7$. What is the solution?

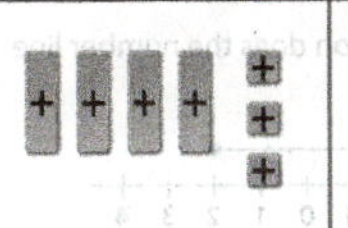

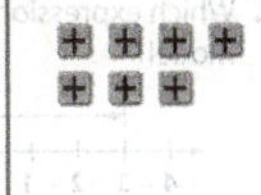

Ⓐ $x = 1$ Ⓒ $x = 10$
Ⓑ $x = 4$ Ⓓ $x = 16$

Mini-Task

7. A taxi costs \$4 plus \$2 per mile driven. Hansel's taxi ride cost \$10 in all.

a. Write an equation that can be used to find m, the number of miles Hansel rode.

$2m + 4 = 10$

b. Model your answer from Part **a** using algebra tiles. Draw the tiles below.

c. How do you solve the equation using tiles? What is the solution?

Remove 4 +1-tiles from each side of the mat. Divide the remaining tiles into 2 equal groups, showing that $m = 3$.

Assessment Readiness

Assessment Readiness Tip A two-step equation uses two operations. You can use numbers, variables, and operations to write two-step equations for real-world problems.

Item 3 Some students may try to begin by translating the first sentence. Remind students to first read the entire problem and analyze what the problem is asking for. Then identify a variable that will answer the question.

Avoid Common Errors

Item 1 Some students forget how to determine which way a number line should be shaded. Remind students that the inequality sign points the direction of the shading. Greater than, >, points right, so will shaded to the right. Less than, <, points left, so will be shaded to the left.

Item 5 After learning about reversing the inequality symbol, some students apply the rule too often, using it whenever they multiply or divide. Remind them to only reverse the inequality symbol when multiplying or dividing both sides by a *negative* number.

Items	Lesson	Mathematical Processes and Practices
1	GR4.5	MP.2, MP.4
2	GR4.1	MP.2, MP.4, MP.8
3	GR4.3	MP.1, MP.2
4	GR4.2	MP.2, MP.4, MP.8
5	GR4.6	MP.2
6	GR4.4	MP.2, MP.4
7	GR4.2, GR4.3, GR4.4	MP.1, MP.2, MP.4, MP.8

Assessment Readiness

Assessment Readiness Tip Integer operations on number lines are often represented by movement, not by endpoints.

Item 2 Often, students will make the mistake of thinking that the expressions derived from number lines are based on where the lines start and end. So, they will write the expression $2 + (-3)$. However, since the line starts at 2 and *moves* five to the left, it should instead be $2 + (-5)$ or $2 - 5$.

Item 5 Based on the numbers, students might incorrectly select the expression $-3 + (-3)$. Remind students that the repetitive movement of equal increments represents multiplication, not addition. The number line shows a movement of 3 units left 3 times, so the expression is $3(-3)$.

Avoid Common Errors

Item 1 Some students have a hard time finding the total price after a tax or discount is applied, because it takes more than one step. Remind students that after calculating the sales tax amount, they have to add the sales tax to the original price or subtract the discount from the original price.

Item 9 Students may be confused by a graph without numbers. Explain to them that although they can't find most of the ordered pairs that lie on the line, they can still see whether the line passes through the origin.

Item 11 Some students forget that ratios can be simplified. Remind students to reduce each fraction to its lowest terms.

UNIT 8

Assessment Readiness

Selected Response

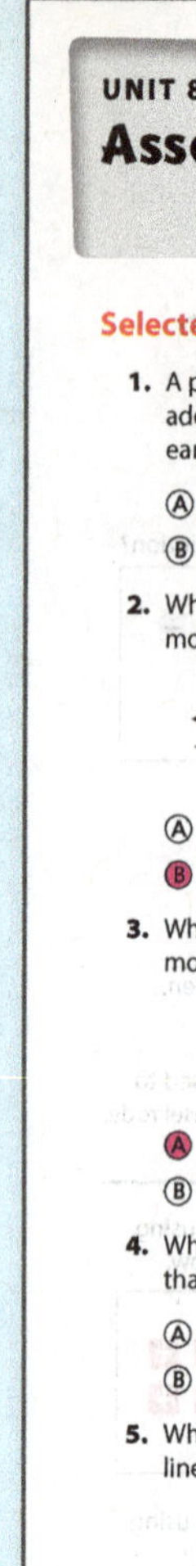

1. A pair of earbuds costs $16.00, plus an additional 6% for sales tax. What do the earbuds cost in all?

   Ⓐ $16.06 Ⓒ $16.66
   Ⓑ $16.60 Ⓓ $16.96

2. Which expression does the number line model?

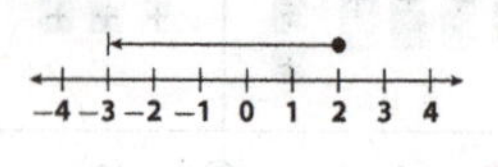

   Ⓐ $2 + 5$ Ⓒ $2 + (-3)$
   Ⓑ $2 - 5$ Ⓓ $-3 + 5$

3. Which factored algebraic expression is modeled by the tiles?

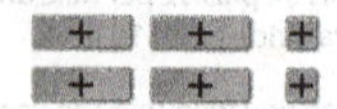

   Ⓐ $2(2x + 1)$ Ⓒ $2(x + 2)$
   Ⓑ $3(x + 1)$ Ⓓ $4(x + 1)$

4. Which addition problem has an answer that is a negative integer?

   Ⓐ $-3 + 4$ Ⓒ $2 + (-2)$
   Ⓑ $2 + 0$ Ⓓ $5 + (-7)$

5. Which expression does the number line model?

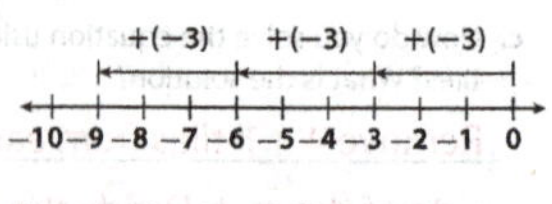

   Ⓐ $-3 + (-3)$ Ⓒ $3(-3)$
   Ⓑ $-9 + 6$ Ⓓ $3(3)$

6. What is $3\left(\frac{2}{5}\right)$?

   Ⓐ $3\frac{2}{5}$ Ⓒ $1\frac{1}{5}$
   Ⓑ 1 Ⓓ $\frac{2}{15}$

7. What is the solution of the inequality $x - 9 > 7$?

   Ⓐ $x > 16$ Ⓒ $x > -2$
   Ⓑ $x < 16$ Ⓓ $x < -2$

8. Which number is equivalent to $\frac{-18}{-2}$?

   Ⓐ $-\frac{18}{2}$ Ⓒ $\frac{18}{-2}$
   Ⓑ $\frac{-18}{2}$ Ⓓ $\frac{18}{2}$

9. Which graph shows a proportional relationship?

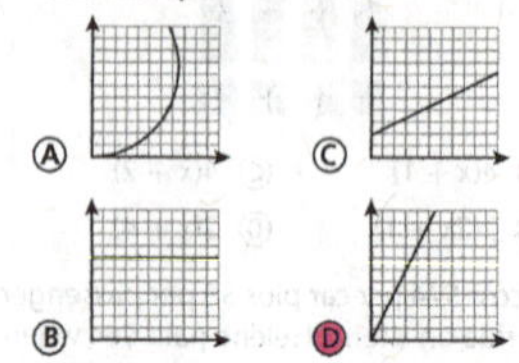

10. Eight avocadoes and a jar of salsa cost $15. The jar of salsa costs $3. Which equation could you use to find a, the cost of one avocado?

    Ⓐ $3a + 8 = 15$ Ⓒ $8a = 18$
    Ⓑ $8a + 3 = 15$ Ⓓ $a + 8 = 18$

11. Which ratios are equivalent?

    Ⓐ $\frac{3}{4}$ and $\frac{4}{3}$ Ⓒ $\frac{1}{2}$ and $\frac{2}{3}$
    Ⓑ $\frac{6}{8}$ and $\frac{9}{12}$ Ⓓ $\frac{4}{5}$ and $\frac{2}{3}$

Items	Lesson	Mathematical Processes and Practices
1	GR3.4	MP.2
2	GR2.3	MP.2, MP.4
3	GR4.1	MP.2, MP.4, MP.8
4	GR1.2	MP.2
5	GR1.3	MP.2, MP.4, MP.8
6	GR2.4	MP.2
7	GR4.5	MP.2
8	GR2.5	MP.2
9	GR3.3	MP.2, MP.3, MP.4
10	GR4.3	MP.1, MP.2
11	GR2.1	MP.2

12. Choose the addition problem that the counters model.

Ⓐ $-2 + (-4)$ (selected)
Ⓑ $-2 + 4$
Ⓒ $2 - 4$
Ⓓ $2 + (-4)$

13. A laser printer prints 80 pages in 4 minutes. What is this printer's unit rate?

Ⓐ 0.05 page per minute
Ⓑ 20 pages per minute (selected)
Ⓒ 76 pages per minute
Ⓓ 84 pages per minute

14. In 2014, the Prairie Dogs won 20 games. The next year, the team improved and won 25 games. What was the percent increase in games won?

Ⓐ 10%
Ⓑ 20%
Ⓒ 25% (selected)
Ⓓ 30%

15. What is the sum of $\frac{1}{2}$ and $-\frac{3}{4}$?

-1 0 1 2

Ⓐ $1\frac{1}{4}$
Ⓑ $\frac{1}{4}$
Ⓒ $-\frac{1}{2}$
Ⓓ $-\frac{1}{4}$ (selected)

16. Mr. Park borrowed $200 for 5 years. He is charged 6% simple interest per year. How much interest will he pay in all?

Ⓐ $60 (selected)
Ⓑ $30
Ⓒ $12
Ⓓ $6

Mini-Task

17. The algebra tiles model an equation.

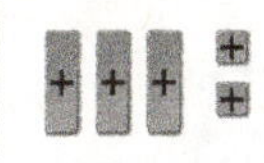

a. Write the equation modeled. Use x as your variable.

$3x + 2 = 8$

b. Solve your equation for x. Explain your steps clearly.

Sample answer: Remove two +1 tiles from each side of the mat. Then divide each side into three equal groups. Since each equal group contains one x tile and two +1 tiles, $x = 2$.

c. The inequality $3x \geq 6$ is related to the equation you just solved. What is the solution to this inequality?

$x \geq 2$

d. How are the solutions in Parts **b** and **c** alike? How are they different?

Both solutions contain the value $x = 2$. But the inequality also includes all values of x greater than 2.

e. Graph your solution from Part **c** on the number line.

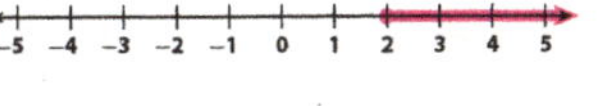

Assessment Readiness

Assessment Readiness Tip Exercises requiring written explanation can be solved first, and then explained later.

Item 17b Sometimes, to properly explain a solution, it is easier to do the math that goes with it. Encourage students to work through the problem first, if need be, then go back and answer the questions once they have worked through the problem.

Avoid Common Errors

Item 15 Some students may forget to account for the negative sign on the $\frac{3}{4}$ and incorrectly choose answer A. Remind students to pay close attention to the sign of each number.

Items	Lesson	Mathematical Processes and Practices
12	GR1.1	MP.2, MP.4
13	GR3.1	MP.1, MP.2
14	GR3.5	MP.1, MP.2
15	GR2.2	MP.2, MP.4
16	GR3.6	MP.1, MP.2
17	GR4.2, GR4.3, GR4.4, GR4.6	MP.1, MP.2, MP.3, MP.4, MP.8